Your Church
Can Be Healthy

Creative Leadership Series

Your Church
Can Be Healthy

C. Peter Wagner

Creative Leadership Series

Lyle E. Schaller, Editor

Abingdon Press / Nashville

YOUR CHURCH CAN BE HEALTHY

Copyright © 1979 by C. Peter Wagner

Fifth Printing 1985

All Rights Reserved
No part of this book may be reproduced in any manner
whatsoever without written permission of the publisher
except brief quotations embodied in critical articles
or reviews. For information address Abingdon Press,
Nashville, Tennessee

Library of Congress Cataloging in Publication Data

WAGNER, C PETER.
  Your church can be healthy.
  (Creative leadership series)
  Includes bibliographical references and index.
  1. Church growth. I. Title. II. Series.
  BV652.25.W33   253'.5   79-974

ISBN 0-687-46870-1

Material in this book has appeared in condensed form in articles which
appeared in *Theology News and Notes* (Pasadena: Fuller Theological Seminary),
October, 1977, pp. 5 ff., under the title, "The Pathology of Church Growth:
Some Introductory Notes," and *Today's Christian* (Pasadena, Fuller Evangelistic Association) in serial form, from July, 1977, through December, 1977, under
the title "Common Diseases in American Churches."

MANUFACTURED BY THE PARTHENON PRESS AT
NASHVILLE, TENNESSEE, UNITED STATES OF AMERICA

Dedicated to

Lee Benuska
Ted Engstrom
Steve Lazarian

Distinguished lay leaders
whom God has called to guide
Lake Avenue Congregational Church
out of sociological strangulation
and on toward winning
thousands of men and women
in the San Gabriel Valley
to Christ

Foreword

Two of the most important characteristics of creative leadership are the foresight to anticipate what tomorrow may bring and the ability to distinguish between symptoms and problems. The loyal followers often tend to respond only to contemporary events. They also often attempt to treat the symptoms of a problem, without seeking to understand the nature of the problem itself. By contrast, the creative leader possesses and nurtures the gift of foresight. The creative leader also has the gift of curiosity. Curiosity is what causes a person to search behind the symptoms, to identify the nature of the basic illness.

A third aspect of creative leadership is the ability to identify the problem by putting a name on it. Whenever people believe they are up against an unnamed or unknown force, or series of factors, they normally have great difficulty in responding to the problem. Once the basic issue has been identified and named, however, people tend to be able to develop creative and productive responses to that problem. During World War I and World War II, everyone in the United States was able to name the enemy. By contrast, throughout the Vietnam conflict of the 1960s, there was a notable lack of agreement on the name of the enemy. Whenever a new star is discovered or a new baby is born or a new disease is identified, everyone feels more comfortable after a name has been placed on the new phenomenon.

A fourth characteristic of a creative leader is the ability to take corrective action after a problem has been identified and named.

This book offers help to church leaders on all four of these points. First, Dr. Wagner offers clear advice for distinguishing between the symptoms of a congregational problem ("the neighborhood is changing" or "our young people are moving away" or "our members are all getting old") and the basic issue or disease itself.

Second, and the most distinctive contribution of this volume, is the author's placing a name on each one of these common congregational diseases. Once the disease has been identified and named, it becomes easier for everyone to deal with it. That includes the terminal illnesses described in chapters two and three. When the members understand that their church is terminally ill, and why that is the diagnosis, it becomes easier for everyone involved to develop a creative response to that fact of life—and death.

Professor Wagner's third major contribution to creative leadership in the churches in this volume is his description of the symptoms of each of these eight common ecclesiastical diseases. This is where the author reinforces the foresight of the leaders. If the leaders can read the symptoms in time, they can understand what is happening before irreversible decline sets in in that church. The symptoms described by the author offer a means for church leaders to exercise their gift of foresight.

Finally, and this is the most valuable contribution of this volume, Dr. Wagner offers a variety of practical steps to take to combat these diseases. In other words, this book goes beyond analysis and diagnosis; it prescribes a series of responses, treatments, and in most cases, cures, which are tailored for each disease that is identified.

On an average day in the United States and Canada, eight congregations die. A few of these are "swallowed up" into other healthier (or what appear to be healthier) congregations

through mergers, but many simply dissolve. Most denominations estimate it costs them between $50,000 and $250,000 to
give birth to a new congregation. Thus if the death rate due to
curable diseases could be cut in half, and new life could be
breathed into these sick churches, the saving would amount to
at least $70 million annually. While churches exist to save
souls, not to save money or to make money, these figures do
suggest, in secular terms, why this is an important book. Good
stewardship of the resources God has given us requires
creative leaders to exercise the freedom God also has given us,
to take preventive action in time!

Diagnosis, foresight, prescription, implementation, and
stewardship of resources are themes which run through every
volume in this series. They are among the attributes which we
are seeking to nourish in the creative leaders of the churches!

Lyle E. Schaller

Yokefellow Institute
Richmond, Indiana

Contents

Introduction

I wish I didn't have to write this book. I wish churches were never sick. But they are, and my next wish is that the sick ones will recover, regain health and vitality, and grow for the glory of God.

This book describes eight diseases that churches frequently contract. They are not gimmicks designed to prove some point or other—they are maladies which occur in churches with significant frequency. The descriptions of these diseases have been tested with hundreds of church leaders from most American denominations, and they seem to ring true. They are recognizable by pastors, church officers, and concerned Christian people.

This book is only a beginning. I hope that the field of church pathology will develop over the next few years into an increasingly sophisticated body of knowledge which will be useful in identifying and removing obstacles to church growth.

The objective of this book is to help fulfill the Great Commission. As I understand the Scriptures, every Christian is to make his or her contribution to the process of "making disciples of all nations." One of God's important instruments to accomplish this is the local church. But local churches with ill health can hardly do all that God wants them to do in winning the lost around them to Jesus Christ. Knowing what is wrong with churches is an important step toward good health and vigorous growth.

There is no sense of finality in what I have written. These diseases have been tested only in American churches, mostly Anglo-American churches. How many of the diseases are common among churches in other cultures, I do not yet know, although I hope eventually to find out. Fresh work in the pathology of churches needs to be done in every nation and in the midst of every people. Many helpful insights remain to be discovered.

So this book is admittedly tentative and cautious. The concepts will be refined and corrected and supplemented by perceptions much sharper than mine. Meanwhile, I hope that if your church is healthy and growing, you may get some insights here as to what to avoid in the future. If it has growth problems, it is my prayer that God will use this book to help you understand what is wrong and take the steps necessary to correct it.

I.

Can the
Body of Christ
Be Sick?

The Bible calls the church the "body of Christ." Both Ephesians 1:22, 23 and Colossians 1:18 say that Jesus is the head of the church, which is his body.

Now I fully realize that biblical analogies should not be pushed too far. But in my research on the growth and nongrowth of churches here in America and around the world, I soon discovered that some churches in their present condition apparently cannot grow. I kept asking the question Why?

It seems that one of the signs of good church health is growth. If it is faithful to the Lord, and if it is in a healthy condition, he will add "to the church daily such as should be saved," as he did in that very healthy church planted in Jerusalem on the day of Pentecost (Acts 2:47). But some churches which are faithful do not seem to grow. They confess Jesus as Lord. They believe sound doctrine. They pray with fervor. They study the Bible and seek to obey its precepts. They raise funds for foreign missions. They serve fellow human beings. They celebrate the Lord's Supper with regularity. But somehow their faithfulness alone does not seem to be attractive enough to outsiders to draw them into the church.

Over the past decade or so, membership losses in key American denominations have been startling. The United Methodist Church alone has lost nearly 1.2 million members from their church rolls and over 2 million from their Sunday schools. The United Presbyterian Church has lost over one-half million. The Episcopal Church, the Disciples of Christ, the United Church of Christ, the Presbyterian Church U.S., and numbers of others have found themselves in a period of declining membership.

If every denomination in America had been losing over the last decade, that would be one thing. But while some churches were declining, others were growing. The Southern Baptists added about 2 million members over that same period. The Assemblies of God, Baptist General Conference, Christian and Missionary Alliance, Seventh-day Adventists, Church of God (Cleveland), Church of the Nazarene, and numbers of others grew steadily.

What is the difference?

Church Growth Is Complex

Church growth is always complex. A recent high-level symposium was convened by the Hartford Seminary Foundation to study the decline of churches in the major denominations.[1] One of their discoveries after two years of work was that churches grow and decline as a result of the interplay of four basic sets of factors.

1. *National Contextual Factors.* These relate to national trends in population, attitudes, values, and social conditions.

2. *National Institutional Factors.* These relate to policies determined on the denominational level concerning priorities of ministry, theological stance, church polity, and other areas that to some degree affect all the churches in the denomination.

3. *Local Contextual Factors.* This relates to social trends in the local neighborhood or area where the church is located.

4. *Local Institutional Factors.* These are conditions that exist among the leadership and membership of the local church.

The focus of this book will be primarily on local institutional factors and secondarily on local contextual factors. The other sets have a bearing on pathology, but our purpose is to analyze growth and nongrowth from the point of view of the health of the local church, not the national denomination or judicatory.

This brings us back to the "body of Christ." As far as we know from the Bible, Jesus Christ was never sick while he was on earth. But there is no theological reason to suppose that he couldn't have been sick at some time or other. Christians believe that Jesus was fully human, while also being fully divine. Of course, he did not sin, and some might argue that this could have kept him from being sick. We do not know that, for sure.

In any case, the body of Christ today—the church—is not free from sin. Nor is it free from sickness. I do not believe that we stretch the biblical analogy too far to suppose that the body of Christ can be sick, or it can be healthy. One of the indications of this is that while the membership of the United Methodist denomination, for example, was declining severely, many local United Methodist churches were growing vigorously. Obviously, some of their churches are healthy and some are sick. The same could be said about the other denominations.

Our concern is to discover and describe the reasons.

The Medical Model

The notion of relating church growth to church health has been proving helpful to many church leaders. It is not entirely new. Many in the past have spoken of healthy or sick churches as being characterized by certain traits. Some have coined disease-like names to prove a point they were making. Some have accused a church that feels new buildings are necessary for growth of having an "edifice complex." Hollis L. Green has written a whole book entitled *Why Churches Die*. It has 35 chapters, each describing a possible cause of decline in a given local church.

But up until now, there has been no systematic and sustained effort that I know of to develop what we are calling the field of church pathology. Diseases had not been identified, named, and analyzed. Finding a name for a disease in itself can begin a curing process called the "Rumplestiltskin effect" by some. Just knowing what is wrong with you removes the mystery and brings a therapeutic influence.

The pathology of church growth has not been included in most seminary and Bible school curriculums in the past. There may not be a single minister in America who has taken a course in the subject. As a result, pastors tend to know very little about the field, and their churches may be sick without their realizing it. Or they may suspect that their church is sick, but are not able either to diagnose the disease or to prescribe a cure.

One of the encouraging signs is the recent emergence of a cadre of professional church diagnosticians whom I would like to call "ecclesiologists." A combination of aptitude, training, and intuition has given these persons the ability to examine a church and diagnose its health in approximately one day's time, given some previous research and measurements by the pastor.[2] Some of these ecclesiologists work out of denominational offices and some are interdenominational. My hope is that within five to ten years they will be almost as readily available to churches as physicians are to people in general. If so, massive declines in church membership such as we have mentioned should be a thing of the past.

As the field of church health in relationship to church growth develops, pastors themselves will gain a sensitivity to the conditions of their own churches and will be able to diagnose many of the diseases themselves. The younger ones will be studying this in seminary and Bible school, as textbooks for such a study appear. The older ones will pick up professional training in the doctor of ministry and continuing education programs that are now proliferating in America.[3]

The Positive Side: Vital Signs

When a body is functioning in a healthy way, its vital signs are in good shape. This is the positive side of health. Churches, like human beings, have vital signs that seem to be common among those that are healthy and growing. If the vital signs are known, efforts to maintain them can be made in order to avoid illness. This is the preventive medicine aspect of church health. Healthy churches resist disease. It is much more advisable to prevent an illness than to contract one and have to cure it.

While undoubtedly much more needs to be done in the field, I have made an attempt to analyze seven of the vital signs of healthy churches in my book, *Your Church Can Grow*.[4] Here is a brief review of them before we begin the negative side, that of pathology:

1. The pastoral leadership is the first vital sign of a healthy church. Because I will have more to say about the pastor later on in this chapter, I will not elaborate here.

2. A well-mobilized laity is another vital sign. While there are many ways that laity can be mobilized, I do not believe that any can improve on what are described in the Bible as spiritual gifts. Christians are to function as members of Christ's body, and each one has been given a spiritual gift or gifts to do a certain job. Therefore, one of the most important spiritual exercises for a Christian is to discover, develop, and use his or her spiritual gift.

Not only does knowing one's spiritual gift or gifts benefit each individual Christian, but it also provides all the resources necessary for a church to grow. Because church growth is complex, mobilizing spiritual gifts is not by itself sufficient to make any church grow, but it certainly is a factor of first-line

21

priority. Just how the mobilization of 27 spiritual gifts relates to growth dynamics in churches is developed in my book, *Your Spiritual Gifts Can Help Your Church Grow*,[5] so I need not expand further on the matter here.

3. The third vital sign is that the church is big enough to provide the kind of services that meet the needs of the community. A church, in order to be attractive to newcomers, has to meet the needs of its members well. If it does, it will have satisfied customers, so to speak, and they will spread the news that their church is doing things that appeal to outsiders, as well. Some things can be done in churches of any size, such as bringing people to Christ, providing fellowship and pastoral care, or offering Sunday school training for young children. But other kinds of services require a larger "critical mass" in order to generate appeal. A strong ministry to single adults, for example, requires substantial numbers in order to be attractive. One of the slogans used by experts in this field is "Singles go where singles are." A church of 200 or 300 is probably not going to have a dynamic singles ministry, so if ministering to singles is a community need the church wants to meet, it must be fairly large to do an adequate job.

Some churches find small, quiet worship services satisfying. A congregation of 150 with few or no strangers, and a choir of 25 seems just right to many Christians. Others feel that Sunday morning should be more of an event, with several hundred or thousands present, traffic problems in the neighborhood, choirs and orchestras, and perhaps television cameras. If the former is desired, almost any size church can do it. If it is the latter, however, a church of 500 or even 1,000 may not be big enough.

It is recommended that a church carefully examine the needs of the unchurched people around them, establish a philosophy of ministry that will meet those needs, and plan to grow until it is large enough to conduct that sort of ministry adequately.

4. The fourth vital sign has to do with what could be called

the "internal organs" of the body of Christ. The way people are grouped together in a church has a good deal to do with its growth. Three basic groupings need to be considered in order to find the right balance for a given church in a given situation. The largest is the membership group, which can be almost any size; the middle one is the fellowship group, which should be somewhere around 40 to 120; and the smallest is the spiritual kinship group, which is limited to 8 to 12 persons. I like to call these three structures "celebration," "congregation," and "cell."

Smaller churches frequently plateau at around 200 members, because they have not developed a system for separating internal fellowship or congregations. If these are not separated, little growth can be expected. Larger churches may plateau if their internal fellowship groups develop individual growth problems, but this difficulty is frequently invisible to the leadership. Lyle Schaller has provided many valuable insights into this vital sign in his writings, for example, pages 69 through 98 in his *Assimilating New Members*.

5. Growing churches find that their members come basically from one kind of people. This does not mean that they are racist, or that their doors are closed to anyone who wants to come to their church, worship with them, or take out membership. It does mean that they have a program that is meeting the spiritual needs of one specific kind of people, and that there is no way one local church can do a good job of meeting the needs of all different kinds of people.

This has become one of the most controversial principles associated with the Church Growth Movement. However, it is directly related to two of the diseases we will be discussing later, so I will postpone further comment.

6. The sixth vital sign is so obvious that it hardly has to be mentioned, but it is an evangelistic method that has proven effective in making disciples. By definition, if a church is growing, unless the growth is all biological and transfer growth, something evangelistic is working. Evangelistic

methodologies are so diverse that no one method can be recommended as superior to others. Each church has to come up with a method that will bring people to Christ and also unite them in fellowship with other Christians. Those churches that do, grow.

7. Priorities properly arranged in biblical order constitute the seventh vital sign. Often this involves the set previously called the "national institutional factor." That is, some denominational bureaucracies have made priority decisions for their constituents that have been a definite contributing factor to church decline. This will be discussed again in the final chapter.

Four Axioms of Church Growth

Before we move on to the specific diseases a church may become infected with, we need to look at four preconditions to growth. As you will see, they are derived partially from the seven vital signs of a healthy church, but their focus is slightly different, and they also pinpoint the essentials. A church can score well on 4 or 5 of the 7 vital signs and perhaps grow, if it has an exceptionally strong growth mix. But a church cannot score low on any of these axioms and expect to grow well.

Axiom 1: The pastor must want the church to grow and be willing to pay the price.

As we hinted above in the first vital sign, the pastor is the person who is key to the growth of the local church. Some may hold certain theological points of view which would question whether this is the way things ought to be, but accumulating evidence continues to confirm that it is a fact. I have yet to see a growing church in which the pastor does not want the church to grow and is not willing to pay the price.

Doesn't every pastor want his or her church to grow? The answer to this is no. Larry Richards recently did a national survey of 5,000 pastors randomly selected by computer, testing their attitudes on various issues. He found that less than half gave high priority to "planning and implementing church growth."

It is true that church growth is onerous to certain people. Some pastors were trained in seminary not to go for growth in their ministry. They believe that "small is beautiful," and that nongrowing churches are characterized by quality. They prefer quality to quantity, so vigorous growth is to be avoided.

Growth to some is undignified. As Howard L. Rice of San Francisco Theological Seminary puts it:

> For traditional main-line Protestant denominations the whole subject of confronting the world . . . with the Good News of Jesus Christ is thought of as unseemly or in poor taste. With relatively few exceptions, the whole matter of winning persons for Christ is viewed as something for the "unwashed" sect groups. . . .[6]

Even when some pastors say they want growth, they are not willing to pay the price. Church growth does not come cheaply, and therefore, every pastor cannot handle it. Pastors who wish to count the cost of growth need to take four things into consideration.

A. They must be willing to work hard. Pastoring a church that is growing rapidly is much more difficult than pastoring a declining church. In fact, a declining church gets easier to pastor every year. Long hours, large expenditures of energy, and a heavy burden of responsibilities await a pastor whose church begins to grow well.

B. They must be willing to take the training. While growth leadership comes intuitively to some with special spiritual gifts, advanced training in the area of church growth will make all the difference in the world to most. However, the training costs money, it takes time, and it requires self-discipline.

C. They must be willing to share leadership. Some pastors are so constituted that they feel they must do all the work themselves. They have little or no inclination to share leadership either with professional staff or with the laity. While there may be nothing wrong with this, it should be frankly evaluated as a limitation to the growth of the church.

D. They must be willing to have members they cannot pastor personally. In a church of up to 200 members one pastor can give fairly adequate attention to the pastoral needs of the whole flock. Beyond that, capacities are stretched, and if vigorous growth continues, there is no way a one-on-one relationship can be maintained with all church members. Pastoral attention will have to be provided by someone else. This is too high a price for some pastors to pay, so they avoid growth as much as possible.

Axiom 2: The people must want the church to grow and be willing to pay the price.

While the pastor may be the key person for growth, if the people are not motivated, it will not happen. After all, the church is not a building or an institution; ultimately, it is people. Some of my worst experiences come from telephone calls from pastors who have taken church-growth training, have gone back to their churches full of enthusiasm, and have been stopped cold by an obstinate board of deacons or session or vestry. Frustration levels run high, because the pastors know that if they do not stimulate goal ownership on the part of the lay leaders of the church in one way or another, dreams for church growth cannot be fulfilled.[7]

The price a congregation has to pay for growth differs somewhat from that of the pastor. It has at least three dimensions:

A. The people must accept the pastor's leadership. In many churches the pastor is not expected to be a leader. A group of lay people have accumulated a certain kind of seniority in the church, and the church is in their hands. Pastors come and go; they are expected to serve as ecclesiastical housekeepers. They preach sermons, baptize, marry the young, and bury the dead. Pastoral tenure is set at four to six years by unwritten law. This assures the church fathers and mothers that their control will not be threatened. By arranging this, they have constructed an effective system for nongrowth.

B. The church members must be willing to provide the funds for growth. Most church growth in America is expensive. I personally see nothing wrong in this. Church members could spend their money on things much less noble than winning their friends and neighbors to Christ. But the willingness to give is usually a necessity for growth. For example, as I write this, my own church, Lake Avenue Congregational Church, has decided to build a new sanctuary to handle the people God has given it in recent years. The price tag is $5.5 million, which must come from donations over and above regular giving during the next three years. The rule of thumb that has been proposed is for members to calculate their net worth, and give 10 percent of it over a three-year period. That is not an easy commitment to make, but no one said that winning people to Christ in Pasadena, California, is easy. My wife, Doris, and I have decided to do our part and trust God for the 10 percent. Hundreds of other members are doing the same. Result: growth is a possibility.

C. They must be willing to sacrifice fellowship for growth. For many church members, this is the most difficult part of the price to pay. When a growing church begins to pass the 200 to 300 mark, more and more strangers are noticed in the worship service. The church is no longer one happy family where everyone knows everyone else. Fellowship has to take place in several subgroups rather than among the membership group as a whole. And if the church is to continue to grow well, the fellowship groups have to be prepared to divide regularly. Some people dislike this idea so much they refuse to support goals for growth. If enough refuse, the church won't grow.

Axiom 3: The church must agree that the goal of evangelism is to make disciples.

I have seen churches in which the pastor is gung ho for growth, the congregation is with him, the budget is available, but still no growth happens. One reason may be that the

27

evangelistic program of the church is geared to getting people to make "decisions for Christ," rather than to become responsible disciples. Decisions for Christ are important, but they are only part of the story. Each person who makes a commitment to Christ should be encouraged to make a simultaneous commitment to the body of Christ. This, I believe, is soundly biblical. It is also practical and necessary for church growth.

Axiom 4: The church must not have a terminal illness.

The concept of a church with a terminal illness has not been widely articulated in Christian circles. But it is an all too common phenomenon. We have no way of knowing how many of the 290,000 Protestant churches in America might have a terminal illness. One recent study, however, showed that between 3 and 6 percent of the 35,000 Southern Baptist churches have a terminal disease. If this figure were true nationwide, it would mean that perhaps 15,000 are about to expire.

Churches die hard. Many of them go out kicking and screaming, so to speak, and bring little blessing to the kingdom of God. However, this is not necessary. If churches with terminal illnesses find out about them early enough and face the situation realistically, they can die with dignity. I once heard Wendell Belew of the Southern Baptist Home Mission Board say somewhat lightly that the next department they create there ought to be a "Department of Euthanasia." I didn't know what to make of it at first, but the more I have thought about it, the more I think such a department might end up as a great asset to God's kingdom.

Churches with terminal illnesses cannot die with dignity if they do not know what is happening to them. As far as I know, there are two common terminal illnesses, ethnikitis and old age. The other six diseases are serious but not necessarily terminal. It is time now to describe them all.

II.

Ethnikitis:
Should We Move Out Now?

Ethnikitis is one of the two terminal illnesses of churches. It is mentioned first because it is undoubtedly the most ruthless killer of churches in America today. Ethnikitis is the terminal disease mentioned in chapter 1 that has been discovered in between 1,600 and 2,000 Southern Baptist churches alone. In Baltimore, for example, over 50 percent of Southern Baptist churches have ethnikitis. Probably no denomination is exempt.

Many books on the contemporary religious situation in America recognize the problem of ethnikitis, although that label is my own invention and other names are used. In their excellent book, *How to Grow a Church,* Donald McGavran and Win Arn call it "the changing church." Carlisle Driggers calls it "the church in the changing community," in his book of the same name. Some authors admit that the situation is terminal, but many of them—unrealistically, in my opinion—attempt to suggest cures.

Ethnikitis is beyond the control of the local church that contracts it. Once it sets in, the church can control its reaction to it, but the disease cannot be reversed. It is not a "local institutional factor," to use the terminology introduced in chapter 1. It is a "local contextual factor."

That is why it is probably more accurate to focus attention on the changing *community* rather than the changing *church*. As we shall see, the problem usually revolves around a static church in a changing neighborhood.

The Scenario

The scenario for a church with ethnikitis is familiar to most families who have lived in urban areas in America. The church that gets ethnikitis was once a neighborhood church. It was started among one basic kind of people, namely those who lived in the neighborhood. The church grew and often flourished because the people in the neighborhood were attracted to the church and its congregation. They were perceived as "our kind of people." Their language, their worship styles, their musical tastes, their social activities, and their personal life-styles were compatible.

Then an unanticipated and unprayed-for social phenomenon begins to occur. Other kinds of people begin moving into the neighborhood—just a few at first, then in greater numbers. They seem to enjoy the company of one another more than that of the people already living there. Some of their behavior is strange. It is harder to make friends with them. Their children don't get along too well with the children of the church members. Gradually church families begin moving out of the changing neighborhood and into new neighborhoods where their own life-styles are more generally accepted.

The families who move out, however, are loyal to the church. They have formed close friendships there, they have invested considerable money in the building and program, and they feel at home there on Sundays, even though they don't want to be around the rest of the week. So they commute to the church for services and maintain active membership.

As this process continues, you end up with a church that is virtually an island of one kind of people, in the midst of a community of another kind of people, with very little communication between them. Such a church has ethnikitis. It begins to decline because the people in the neighborhood are not being won, nor are those who commute from a distance able to interest their new friends in the church. Most of their friends prefer to join churches in the area where they live, rather than commute into another neighborhood, especially one increasingly populated with a different kind of people.

Churches with ethnikitis can die in as short a period as five years or less, depending on the rapidity of the population change and the cultural distance between the groups involved. But some can survive for 15 or 20 years. The crunch comes when the children of those who move out reach elementary school age. At this point in life, the parents will usually stop commuting in to the church and join a church where their children will enjoy a Sunday school and church life compatible with their school situation. Meanwhile, the older members whose children are no longer at home will continue in the church, but the age level and death rate among them will continue to increase. By then, gloom and despair have usually set in. The church is no longer the happy, joy-filled place it used to be. One day soon "Ichabod" will sadly be written over the door.

An Epidemic of Ethnikitis

All too many real-life illustrations of ethnikitis can be found. For example, a severe epidemic of ethnikitis swept Southern Baptist churches in Birmingham, Alabama, not too long ago. Between 1966 and 1973, a rapid population shift took place as a result of new conditions created by the civil rights movement. Blacks began moving into white neighborhoods. The Baptist *Home Missions* magazine boldly published a two-page spread in 1975, showing eight graphs of church decline, each one superimposed over a ghost-like photograph of the church facility as it used to be. Of the eight churches that died, seven of them died of ethnikitis. The eighth was a fairly new church

31

which we might say was stillborn. And the article went on to say that 42 more Baptist churches in Birmingham might soon be faced with ethnikitis.

The population change in Birmingham was so radical that three of the churches died in four years. None of them lasted for more than eight years after ethnikitis set in. At their high points the eight churches had a cumulative Sunday school enrollment of 3,060, so the loss was quite substantial. I am not aware of the conditions under which all the churches died. But at least one, Calvary Baptist Church, died with dignity and had a happy celebration when they turned their facilities over to the black Thirteenth Avenue Macedonian Baptist Church.[1]

Austin Congregational Church

A fascinating analysis of a case of ethnikitis is presented by Walter Ziegenhals of the Community Renewal Society of Chicago. It concerns Austin Congregational Church, built in 1926 in the Austin suburb of Chicago, which at that time was a pleasant, quiet, well-scrubbed place for white, upper-middle-class families. The church they built fit their tastes well. It included a gymnasium, a Moeller pipe organ, and even quarters for the custodian. The outreach program was effective, and Austin Congregational Church grew from 360 members in 1927, to 516 in 1950. But in 1950, ethnikitis set in. Ziegenhals says:

> The next 20 years weave a sad and familiar tale of inevitable decline. Older members of the church retire or move away or die. Younger families move to the suburbs. Blacks begin to move into Austin. Community leaders offer sober and reasoned pronouncements about the importance of an integrated community. By 1966 the power structure was accused of fleeing to the suburbs and of not "giving a damn" about Austin Church.

Here is a clear case of a church going out kicking and screaming. When Christian people start swearing at one another, something is seriously wrong. That church had a terminal illness for several years but was not able to cope with it enough to die with dignity. Ziegenhals summarizes the basic principle.

> The history of Austin Church reveals once again that we are not going to be blessed with integrated churches, at least not in the foreseeable future. In communities like Hyde Park, where the University of Chicago generates a continuing supply of whites, that possibility still exists. Changing communities like Austin offer no such hope. The exodus of whites, like the corresponding influx of blacks, is inexorable.[2]

The story of Austin Church does have a happy ending, but I will save that for later.

The examples of Birmingham and Austin both involve blacks moving into white neighborhoods. That is undoubtedly the most frequent cause of ethnikitis in American cities today, with Hispanics moving into Anglo neighborhoods a close second. But it should be noted that obvious racial population changes such as these are not the only causes. Even when race is constant, changes in social status within the race can affect church growth.

Black Ethnikitis

I know, for example, of a black church in a black neighborhood that apparently has ethnikitis. The problem in this case is due to a very important church growth principle described by Donald McGavran in *Understanding Church Growth* as "redemption and lift." Here is how it happened in this church.

The church was started by a popular black preacher in a black community. The Lord blessed his efforts and brought hundreds of people to Christ and to the church through his ministry. The community itself was fairly poor as American communities go. But when men and women found new life in

33

Jesus Christ, not only did they find hope for life eternal, but things began to change in their lives there and then. Broken marriages were patched up. Drunkenness, brawling, and immorality were reduced. Children were loved more. Employers found they had more faithful and efficient employees. Family budgets stabilized, and raises in pay came one after the other. The Christians could afford to give more, and a fine sanctuary was built and packed, Sunday after Sunday.

But while the Christians could afford to give more to their church, and did, they could also afford better automobiles and better homes. Many of them decided to leave their low-cost housing and move to other neighborhoods, some black and some integrated, where they could develop their new life-styles with maximum freedom. Because they recognized that their relationship to Jesus Christ had a great deal to do with their social lift, they remained fiercely loyal to their church. The process happened gradually, and since there was no racial difference involved, they were not accused of indulging in "black flight" or of "not giving a damn" about their neighborhood.

Nevertheless, the church began a steady decline. The upwardly mobile blacks began to lose contact and communication with the blacks who moved into the housing they had vacated. Those in the neighborhood undoubtedly looked with envy at the array of shiny Cadillacs and Lincolns and Oldsmobiles in the parking lot on Sunday mornings. No longer were the people of the church winning friends in the neighborhood around the church and bringing them into their fellowship. The decline will undoubtedly continue until the church dies. It has ethnikitis.

What Is the Solution?

Terminal illnesses, by definition, are incurable. Solutions to the problem may enable the church to die with dignity, however. With one possible exception that we will mention later on, ethnikitis has no cure, so we do well to look into possible alternative solutions. As I see it, there are four.

1. *Die a lingering death.* This is the option that many churches choose when either they refuse to recognize what is happening to them, or when they recognize it but do nothing about it. For example, I can recall talking to the elders of a Presbyterian church here in Pasadena ten years ago and explaining to them that they were going to die of ethnikitis (although the word had not yet been coined). My impression was that they thought I was talking through my hat. Today the congregation has disintegrated, and the building is a community social center, unrelated to the preaching of the gospel.

This obviously is not the recommended solution to the problem.

2. *Adopt a "mission" philosophy of ministry.* The usual situation in a neighborhood that is causing a church to have ethnikitis is that the new people who move in find themselves at a lower socio-economic level than those in the church. In some cases, the new people are definitely hurting, with acute problems of unemployment, marital instability, inadequate housing, lack of legal and medical services, need for recreational facilities, high crime rates, and hunger.

Christian compassion, arising from Christ's command to "love your neighbor as yourself," draws people to want to help those around them. While the people in the community may not be inclined to receive the gospel or join the fellowship of a kind of people with whom they have little in common, they will be grateful for any kind of social help that will alleviate their immediate situation.

Some churches with ethnikitis decide to use their remaining human and financial resources to minister to the social needs of the neighborhood. In most cases, this will not stem the decline in church membership, and the church eventually will die. But this is one of the ways of dying with dignity and ministering in the name of the Lord.

35

3. *Move out.* Moving out of the neighborhood that has changed and into a neighborhood where once again the evangelistic responsibilities of the church can be fulfilled makes sense. It opens the way for growth and for new men and women to find the Savior and be reconciled to God. Many churches with ethnikitis select this option.

The option can be exercised in two ways—through merger or relocation. The congregation can decide to move as a group into an existing church in the new neighborhood, or it can decide to maintain its identity and acquire a sanctuary of its own in a more favorable location. If the latter option is chosen, it might be said that the church does not actually die. In one way a church is people, and a congregation that leaves one sanctuary and enters another does not die. However, as far as the old neighborhood is concerned, the church that used to be there is dead. The ethnikitis was terminal.

4. *Make a transition.* In my opinion, making a clean transition to a church relevant to the new community is the best way to die with dignity. It can be likened to a complete blood transfusion—get rid of the old blood and introduce new blood.

This process is not easy. Tom Roote, the Baptist executive who is working with churches in Birmingham that have ethnikitis, agrees that "it is difficult for churches to acknowledge that they may have to go out of business." He tells of one pastor who had an inkling that his church might be terminally infected, so Roote suggested that they plan to close the church down. Roote says, "He just couldn't bring himself to do it. We're success-oriented in business, in every area; that's churches too."

Some object to this option on theological or ethical grounds. They feel that rather than make transitions, churches should integrate with the people moving into the community. This view, however, is losing strength among church people, even those on the liberal side of the fence who have advocated it most strongly in the past. An editorial in *Christian Century*, for example, says,

Major Protestant denominations are coming to realize that if they are going to continue to have a presence in the city, it will be in the form of black or Hispanic churches.

In the 50s and early 60s the "integrated church" was widely viewed as an embodiment of the ideal of Christian unity, one that was worth seeking and possible to achieve. In the 70s sober realism has set in, and the "integrated church" that goes beyond tokenism is seen as a very temporary fixture on the religious landscape—a "church in transition" from white to non-white.[3]

Back now to Austin Congregational Church. It died in 1969. But in 1973, four years later, the United Church of Christ decided to enter into an important agreement with a large black Baptist church. Ziegenhals says it should have been done at least two years earlier. In my opinion, it probably should have been done eight to ten years earlier, when the Christians in the church started swearing at each other. But better late than never.

Together they decided to form a new black congregation called the Austin Baptist United Church of Christ. The U.C.C. would provide the building and the finances. The Baptists would provide an experienced pastor and a nucleus of ten laypeople. Within three years, the tiny nucleus had grown to a membership of 160 with an average of 70 in attendance at Sunday morning worship. This is excellent church growth because once again Austin Church is ministering to, and attracting neighborhood people to, a neighborhood congregation.

Making the Transition

As I see the transition process, it should be initiated ideally by the white congregation (to use the white-black situation as an example) before it dies, not left to its heirs, as in the case of Austin. Definite plans should be laid to make the transition by a specified date. As a missiologist, I see the process as similar to "indigenizing" the church, or turning it over to the nationals. In this case the "missionaries" are the white church leaders, and the "nationals" the blacks who have moved in.

One year or so before the transition date, a black co-pastor should be hired. If a nucleus of ten laypeople can come along, all the better. The evangelistic outreach thrust for the entire year should be to the black people who live in the neighborhood of the church. By the end of the year, the majority of church members should be black. But whether it is a majority or not, the transition date should be faithfully kept, and a celebration service of transfer should be held.

At that time the white co-pastor resigns and moves on. All white church officers resign and black church officers are installed. The membership can continue to be integrated, of course, for as long as desired, but not the leadership, for at least two years. At the end of two years, any remaining white members are once again eligible for election to church office. But by this time, if they are elected, they will become white officers of a black church.

I realize that this solution may be drastic. It requires a higher than average trust in the Holy Spirit and his ability to work through the new people for the glory of God. The tendency of many is to be chicken-hearted and continue to stretch out the process. I do not recommend it. We are talking about major surgery, and the sooner it is performed the better. The more complete the blood transfusion, the higher will be the future evangelistic power of the church in the new community.

One outstanding example of a kind of transition occurred in Kansas City in 1973. Trinity Baptist Church, a white Southern Baptist congregation, got a severe case of ethnikitis. Blacks were moving into the neighborhood, and the "white flight" was on with a vengeance. Trinity Church decided to die with dignity. Its membership had become so scattered in the suburbs that there was little chance of a successful relocation, so the congregation decided to dissolve. When it did, it donated its attractive $175,000 building to a struggling black congregation, Spruce St. Matthews Baptist Church. In less than two years, attendance at Spruce St. Matthews rose from 100 to 500. Excellent church growth! The death of Trinity became a blessing to the kingdom of God.

There is some biblical teaching also about death with dignity. Jesus said, "Unless a grain of wheat falls into the earth and dies, it remains alone; but if it dies, it bears much fruit" (John 12:24 RSV).

Problems of Immigrant Churches

Before leaving the discussion of ethnikitis, a related problem which might be called "maladaptation" needs to be mentioned in passing. Many churches brought to America by certain groups of immigrants have discovered growth problems after 30 to 50 years of reasonably good health. The Evangelical Covenant Church, the North American Baptists, the Moravians, the Reformed Church in America, the Baptist General Conference, the Lutheran Church Missouri Synod, and many others have problems that the United Methodists and the Southern Baptists and the Pentecostal Holiness and the National Baptists, for example, do not have.

The Evangelical Covenant Church used to be the Swedish Covenant Church. The North American Baptists used to be the German Baptists. The Reformed Church in America used to be the Dutch Reformed, and so forth. These churches enjoyed growth in America as long as there were people from Sweden or Germany or Holland who were relatively new in America. They perceived those churches to be "our kind of people," and they could hear and accept the message of Jesus Christ that came from those churches.

But immigration patterns shift. Swedes and Germans and Dutch are relatively meltable people in America. Give them a few generations, and they are assimilated into the dominantly Anglo-American culture. They no longer want ethnic churches, and in fact they are slightly repulsed by them. To the extent that the church retains its Swedishness or its

39

Germanness or its Dutchness it will decline, because newer immigrants in America today are predominantly from other races and more distinct cultures. Hispanics and Koreans and Filipinos and French and Arabs are not nearly as meltable into the Anglo-American culture as were the northern and western Europeans who dominated our former immigration patterns.

Churches that have remained ethnic too long and are experiencing growth problems as a result, are not terminal. They simply need to adapt and become Anglo-American churches, in most cases. One outstanding example of this is a Reformed Church in America in Orange County, California. Its founding pastor, Robert Schuller, is pedigreed Dutch, and not only was born of the "right" parents, but attended the "right" schools, and married the "right" woman. But when he was assigned the task of starting a church in Orange County some twenty years ago, he found very few Dutch people there. So he decided to call the church Garden Grove Community Church and relegate the Reformed Church in America to a footnote in the church bulletin. As an authentic Orange County kind of Anglo-American church, it has now grown to over 9,000 members, most of whom could care less about Calvin's *Institutes* or the Synod of Dort.

Predictably, Robert Schuller has taken severe criticism over the years from members of the denomination. But, although saddened by their lack of understanding, he has weathered it and has been a great blessing to tens of thousands through his church and the television ministry. If someone different had come and insisted on starting a Dutch church in Orange County, the pastor might well be struggling today with a little congregation of 150, gaining perhaps two or three new families a year.

Growing churches authentically reflect the culture of the community in which God has placed them. Churches with cases of maladaptation need to see what steps can be taken to shed immigrant trappings and become American, if they desire to grow and win new people to Christ.

III.

Old Age:
When Are Life-Support
Systems Called For?

Human geriatrics has developed into a difficult but dignified profession. Church geriatrics is equally difficult, but not nearly as dignified. Because of the institutional nature of a church, old age and death have often been regarded as occurrences which could be caused only by a lack of faithfulness to God, or ministerial incompetence, or both.

Can death come "naturally" to a church? Yes.

Old age, as we will define it in this chapter, leads to a natural death. It is similar to ethnikitis in that the conditions that cause it are beyond the control of church members, pastors, or even bishops. Both old age and ethnikitis are caused by "local contextual factors," or changing community conditions, that are due much more to sociological causes than to anything that happens or does not happen within the church itself.

This sets these two terminal illnesses off from the other six which in themselves are not necessarily terminal. The other six diseases are due mostly to "local institutional factors," not "local contextual factors," to use terms which were discussed in chapter 1.

Ethnikitis is basically an urban disease. It usually occurs in urban neighborhoods, both inner urban and outer urban. It rarely is a problem in rural settings. Old age, on the other hand, is almost invariably rural. It will set in when people move out of an area, and no one moves in. The end result is not a new kind of people in an older neighborhood, but no neighborhood at all. In some urban disaster areas, such as South Bronx, this has happened, but nationwide it is not nearly as common as the dwindling of rural communities.

Senior Citizens

The church disease we are calling old age must not be confused with merely an advanced age level among the church members. The percentage of senior citizens in a congregation may have nothing to do with church old age. In fact, some churches made up of senior citizens are not ill at all—they show superb vitality. For example, there is a United Methodist church in a Southern California community called Leisure World that is healthy and vigorous. It is meeting people's needs and growing. But because no one under 52 is allowed to live in Leisure World, no one under 52 belongs to the church.

In my opinion, the number of churches having programs designed specifically for senior citizens needs to be multiplied in many parts of America today. Demographic statistics have been telling us for some time that the quantity of people of retirement age is increasing in a dramatic manner, and that plans need to be made now, in all segments of society, to cope with these changing conditions. While it is true that many senior citizens will be cared for in existing churches which embrace the entire age span of society, it is equally true that many senior citizens are not, and will not be, touched by present churches. Large numbers of them could be won, however, by new churches that are geared specifically to their needs.

This special kind of church needs to have, first of all, pastoral leadership uniquely equipped for the task. In most cases it requires a mature person as a leader. The worship style, the hours of services, the social activities, the music, the evangelistic program, and all other activities should be tailor-made for older people.

Two myths need to be dispelled if this sort of ministry is to be developed. The first is the myth that older people are anxious to spend a lot of time with younger people. Occasional contact and a smattering of mixed social events, yes. A steady diet, no. The second is the myth that older people cannot easily be won to Christ. Any person who has needs that Jesus can meet can be won to Christ, and senior citizens in America have more than their share of such needs.

A senior citizens' church can grow. The secret of success for churches, Robert Schuller says, is to find a need and fill it, or find a hurt and heal it. Literally millions of senior citizens in America are hurting and can be won to Christ by churches that specialize in ministry to them.

What "Old Age" Is

If a church with many senior citizens is not necessarily a church with the disease of old age, what, then, is the disease?

The disease is more of a community problem than a church problem, although it affects the church just as it affects businesses, schools, public services, housing, and other community institutions. Up until 1970, the general trend in America was away from the farm, out of the country, and to the city. Urban areas grew, while rural areas declined in population. Since 1970, there has been an unanticipated shift in this trend, so that some rural districts are now seeing population growth at the expense of cities.

Still, many rural towns and villages, most of which have churches in them, are disappearing. When this occurs, there is little chance that a church can grow in any of the three ways that churches add members—by biological, transfer, or conversion growth.

Churches can't grow biologically, because the children of the believers do not stay in town. They usually go off to school, get married, and find work in a distant city. They can't grow by transfer, because Christian people looking for a new church are not moving into these towns. And conversion growth possibilities are slim, because many of our declining rural towns are adequately churched, and few unchurched people remain to respond to the gospel.

Old age in churches differs from old age in human beings, in that it is not inevitable. Unless something else takes them first, all human beings will die of old age sooner or later. Not churches, however. The Mar Thoma Church in India, for example, has continued since it was started by the Apostle Thomas in the first century, if we are to believe the historical traditions. Many churches go through a life cycle of growth and decline (discussed under the disease called St. John's Syndrome in chapter 9). Do not confuse the two. Old age is caused by problems in the community around the church, while St. John's Syndrome, as we shall see, is caused by problems in the church itself.

Cego, Texas

Perhaps the best way to clarify the distinction is to give an illustration of a classic case of old age in a church. This one comes from Cego, Texas, a community so small that I still have not been able to find it on a map of the Lone Star State.

The town of Cego was founded a generation ago by a group of 100 German immigrant farmers. They had no desire to assimilate into the Anglo-American culture, so they set up their own community 30 miles away from the nearest town. They maintained their old-country customs and developed a self-contained agricultural system. Each family had a few acres they farmed by hand. They grew their own vegetables, raised their own animals for meat, and produced their own milk, cheese, and eggs. They sold a few melons nearby for the little cash their simple life-style required.

The German farmers were good Christians. They planted a new church when they established Cego. My friend Paul Rutledge, who told me of this interesting case of old age, pastored their church for two years while he was a student in seminary. At first it had been a United Church of Christ. Then they called a Brethren pastor, so it became a Brethren church. Later a Methodist pastor came, and it was a Methodist church. Finally they settled on the name "Cego Church," so they could call any pastor without changing the name again. My friend happened to be a Southern Baptist.

When Paul Rutledge arrived, he discovered that only two people in Cego were not church members. As a good Southern Baptist preacher, however, he took that evangelistic challenge seriously, and before he left he had led one of them to the Lord. His record of reducing the unchurched population of a whole town by 50 percent during a short pastorate is unequaled by most pastors I know!

All the women of Cego had borne children, but every one of them had moved out to go to school or to get jobs elsewhere. None of them had returned to the village of their birth to take up residence. New people found nothing in Cego to attract them, so no one moved in, either. This eliminated possibilities of biological, transfer, or conversion growth, except for the one incorrigible sinner who would not respond to the gospel. When the older people died or became so disabled they could not farm any longer, their land was bought up by the big farmers round about.

It is clear that the Cego Church has a case of old age. It will survive for a time, then it will die.

Zion United Methodist Church

Marissa, Illinois, has a population of 2,464, so it is considerably larger than Cego, Texas. Whether Marissa is disintegrating I do not know, but the story of Zion United Methodist Church there bears telling in the context of old age.

Zion Church, founded in 1868, now has only three members on its rolls. Alex Wildy, 83, and his sister Pearl, 87, keep the church open. It was their mother's dying wish that they do so. At each service, flowers are faithfully placed on their mother's grave.

For the past four years, R. David Reynolds has been parttime pastor of Zion Church. He serves another United Methodist church in Marissa as well. Each week Alex Wildy pays his salary in cash. Wildy himself takes charge of lighting the church's kerosene lamps and stoking the coal stove during the winter months.[1]

While it doesn't supply the answer, the situation at Zion at least raises a question that perhaps many other churches should face realistically. Is this a case of the excessive use of life-support systems?

Meeting the Needs of Dying Churches

Dying churches, like dying people, have special needs that must be met. One of the most fascinating and insightful discussions of the pastoral care required by dying churches comes from William Willimon, a professor at Duke University Divinity School. At one point in his ministry, he had two assignments. He was simultaneously chaplain in a geriatric hospital and pastor of a church with old age. His background and training had prepared him to cope with the situation of the people he was counseling, but not the church he was pastoring.

Pastor Willimon became very frustrated with his church. It had fifty remaining members, and he began to feel that the only reasons for the church's continuing existence were to maintain the church's cemetery and to wait for the members either to die or move away. Every year the budget had to be cut. The members spent a great deal of their energy trying to find somewhere to lay the blame for their decline and in dreaming for some turn of events which would reinstate the "good old days." This was not what Willimon had been taught to expect from a church. He had been programmed to demand growth and change.

One day it occurred to him that his attitudes toward the two institutions he served were inconsistent. When a ninety-year-old person in the hospital died a quiet death, neither he nor the physician felt a sense of failure. They had done everything possible to make the patient physically comfortable and emotionally and spiritually adjusted to the inevitable. Why, then, should he not approach a dying church in the same way? Willimon observes,

> Dying patients may want and need hope, encouragement, absolution, prayer, counseling, hand holding, confession, or a wide variety of pastoral acts. They usually never need the fostering of guilt for their condition or false hopes, scolding, etc.[2]

If these are the needs of terminal people, what do terminal churches require?

I would like to suggest three requirements of churches with old age. Naturally, they are different from the priority needs of healthy churches, but they are no less important, it seems to me, in the total well-being of the kingdom of God.

1. *Guilt removal.* Undoubtedly, the worst symptom a church with terminal old age develops is guilt. It is not difficult to see how this comes about. The American culture is success-oriented. Success for churches has been defined usually as growth. In fact, this is a major theme of persons in the Church Growth Movement, myself included. But I now believe that we have been somewhat hasty in our generalization that any church can grow if it wants to grow. We need to introduce an escape clause into the principle that faithfulness to God demands church growth. We should admit that while this is

true of most churches, it does not apply to churches with terminal illnesses.

Most churches that are not growing ought to feel concerned and take steps to do something about it. But some churches should be relieved of their guilt and allowed to live the rest of their days in peace and comfort. This is why it is not advisable for a district superintendent or a state convention or a bishop to set uniform growth goals for all the churches in the judicatory. Growth goals should be individualized for each church, because local contextual factors vary so much.

What is good growth for some churches might be poor growth for others. Other things being equal, however, the scale that is being used widely for American church growth still applies.

25% per decade	—	poor growth
50% per decade	—	fair growth
100% per decade	—	good growth
200% per decade	—	excellent growth
300% per decade	—	outstanding growth
500% per decade	—	incredible growth

Most churches growing at only 25 percent per decade should be doing better. But churches which, for some reason or other, have been declining rather than growing, can feel successful if they even halt their decline and bottom out for a couple of years. If the church is not growing well because it has a curable disease, the disease should be treated, and the church should move on. But if the disease is terminal, no such unrealistic growth demands should be laid on the church.

How should "success" be viewed in a church dying of old age? "Success," says William Willimon, "will be the successful undertaking of whatever healing, guiding, sustaining, and reconciling acts are needed in a particular situation." The more realistic both pastors and denominational executives are at this point, the better off the body of Christ in general will be.

2. *Honesty in disclosure.* Should the human patient be informed that he or she has a terminal illness? There is no easy answer to this question. In some situations it might be best that the patient does not know. In others, dying with dignity requires that the diagnosis be fully disclosed.

My feeling is that in the case of a church with a terminal illness, the sooner the congregation understands and accepts its condition, the better. This is particularly true when it has ethnikitis, but it also applies to old age. If the terminal condition is successfully dissociated from unfaithfulness to God or from spiritual deficiency or sin, the disclosure can usually be handled with grace.

Of course, it is very important to make sure the diagnosis is accurate. It is possible, for example, to confuse ethnikitis with people-blindness, or old age with St. John's syndrome. But diagnostic procedures for churches have improved a great deal over the past few years, and we can expect them to become more and more refined, and thereby more accurate, in the years to come.[3] Meanwhile, caution is advised before pronouncing a church terminal.

Above all, churches with terminal illnesses should not be pumped up continually with false hopes. Suggestions that if only the church could change pastors or add a Christian education facility or become more involved in community affairs or renovate the sanctuary or hire a minister of music or any number of other things do not help the situation. If the church is going to die, prescribing vitamins or pep pills is not the answer.

3. *Sensitive pastoral care.* Not every physician, or even every psychologist, knows how to handle dying patients well. Not every pastor has the gifts and the sensitivities required to handle a dying church well. For this reason, many pastors may seek a transfer as soon as they begin to suspect that a terminal illness is involved.

But the people in a dying church are still God's people. They are brothers and sisters in Christ to Christians in more fortunate churches. They cannot and ought not to be neglected. Contemporary American culture is often much too quick to relegate handicapped people to asylums and elderly people to rest homes. Our ecclesiastical society is likewise probably too quick to abandon the people in weak and diminishing churches. If we have room for specialists in Christian education and evangelism and visitation and music and worship and youth work, why not specialists in caring for congregations in churches with old age? Perhaps denominational subsidies are needed here, since dying churches frequently have serious budgetary problems.

In any case, sensitive pastoral care is demanded for the people of God caught in America's dying churches. It is, after all, a biblical principle articulated in Galatians 6:2 RSV: "Bear one another's burdens, and so fulfil the law of Christ."

IV.

People-Blindness: Why Isn't Everyone Like Us?

People-blindness, unlike ethnikitis or old age, is not terminal. It can be cured. But, like every disease listed here in the pathology of churches, it retards effective evangelism and stunts the growth of the church. It is necessary, therefore, to recognize it, label it, and understand its symptoms as fully as possible.

There are some churches that seem to be in good health, fully motivated to grow, and active in outreach and evangelism. But their evangelistic efforts do not result in much church growth. Why?

In some cases the trouble lies in the area of what we are calling people-blindness, but because it is a kind of "blindness," the church may not have perceived the problem at all.

E-1, E-2, and E-3

In order to understand people-blindness, it is necessary first to become familiar with some terminology currently being used in the Church Growth Movement. Those who have been trained in church growth or who have been reading church growth literature will be familiar with the designations, E-1, E-2, and E-3.

51

The symbol "E" stands for "evangelism," and the numbers stand for different cultural distances from the person or group initiating the evangelistic process. Thus E-1, or "evangelism-one," signifies evangelism among people of the same culture as the evangelist or the evangelistic team. In contrast, both E-2 and E-3 represent the kind of evangelism necessary to win to Christ people of a different culture from that of the evangelist. E-1 is monocultural evangelism, while E-2 and E-3 are cross-cultural evangelism.

The difference between E-2 and E-3 is a difference in degree only. Both are cross-cultural, but E-3 signifies a culture more radically different from that of the evangelist than E-2. All cultural distances are not equal. This can be illustrated easily by using cultures in different parts of the world as examples. An Anglo-American from Wheaton, Illinois, who went to evangelize the French in a Paris suburb, for example, would be doing E-2 evangelism. French culture is different from Anglo-American culture, but a common Latin and European influence provides many similarities. The same Anglo-American from Wheaton, going to evangelize Buddhists in Thailand, would find himself or herself in an E-3 situation.

But one does not have to leave America to find clear cases of E-2 and E-3 evangelism. An Anglo-American evangelizing Hispanic-Americans would be doing E-2, while evangelizing reservation Navajos would involve E-3.

These distinctions are very important in planning evangelistic strategies. The method appropriate for one is different from that for the others. And there is a clear range of difficulty. E-3 evangelism is the most difficult, E-2 is the next most difficult, and E-1 is the easiest. That is why worldwide, most church growth resulting from one-on-one evangelism is E-1. But E-2 and E-3 are absolutely essential if the gospel is to take root in a new culture. Incidentally, 84 percent of the world's unreached people would require cross-cultural evangelism. Thus, as far as world evangelization is concerned, E-2 and E-3 constitute the highest priority. Once strong, biblical churches are established in a different culture, E-1 evangelism takes over and spreads the gospel.

This is a familiar biblical pattern. To give just one illustration from the New Testament, two separate missions set out to evangelize the city of Antioch. The missionaries in both cases were Jews. In the target city of Antioch, which had a population of 500,000, there were groups of both Jews and Gentiles. The first mission did E-1 evangelism and established churches among Jews only (Acts 11:19). Then about ten years later, another mission was formed that I like to call the C.C.M., the Cyprus and Cyrene Mission. The evangelists of the C.C.M. specialized in E-2 or E-3 evangelism (whichever it might have been to them) in Antioch and began winning the Gentiles and establishing Gentile churches for the first time (Acts 11:20).

Defining People-Blindness

People-blindness is directly related to a lack of understanding of the significant differences between E-1 evangelism on the one hand, and E-2 and E-3 evangelism on the other. The term itself was first introduced by Ralph Winter, of the U.S. Center for World Mission, in his address to the plenary session at the International Congress on World Evangelization, held in Lausanne, Switzerland, in 1974. His topic was "The Highest Priority: Cross-Cultural Evangelism."[1]

We are now ready for a working definition of people-blindness:

People-blindness is the malady which prevents us from seeing the important cultural differences that exist between groups of people living in geographical proximity to one another—differences which tend to create barriers to the acceptance of our message.

Two problems which inhibit the evangelistic process become evident when people-blindness is present.

1. *Problems of transmitting the message.* The most obvious problem in cross-cultural evangelism is linguistic. When languages are mutually unintelligible, the message cannot get

through. But even when the groups involved speak a mutually-intelligible language, dialect differences and many nonverbal forms of communication tend to complicate the transmission of the message. In some cases, prejudice barriers effectively keep the message from getting through.

2. *Problems in "folding" new converts.* In many cases, even if the message gets through, and the person becomes a Christian believer, cultural differences make it virtually impossible to fold that new convert into the fellowship of the church the evangelist belongs to. Some critics find biblical passages that they interpret as saying this ought not to be. Some try to wish it away. But sociologically, it is a fact of life and, as we shall see, if not accepted as a fact, it may shut the door on effective evangelism.

Clearly discernible elements of American social history have made it difficult for many Americans to accept the fact that important differences among subgroupings of American citizens exist. The American dream taught us that our nation is a melting pot and that all Americans are, or soon will be, one culture. Since all Americans have equal rights under the laws of our land, it seems to be a fair conclusion that we all should be one. In that case, all Americans could be reached for Christ by the same methods. And I could expect that anyone, regardless of race, class, national origin, or regional identity would want to join my church if that person becomes a Christian. If my church is good enough for me and my family, it should be good enough for anyone else, too. Such conclusions are typical of those afflicted with people-blindness.

This point of view stresses that since Christ has broken down the middle wall of partition (Eph. 2:14), and that in Christ there is no Greek or Jew or barbarian or Scythian or slave or free (Col. 3:11), people who do have such differences should expect to fit together harmoniously in the same local congregation.

In my opinion, however, those who arrive at such conclusions are reading the Bible with people-blindness. They fail to see the validity of the decisive methods that led to the

54

great E-2 and E-3 evangelistic jumps—first from Hebrew Jews to Hellenistic Jews, then from Jews to Samaritans, then from Jews to Gentiles. In each case, new culturally relevant churches were formed. Conglomerate congregations, as Acts 6:1-7 seems to be teaching us, were generally not feasible. The Judaizers opposed the formation of Gentile churches and wanted all the believers to be culturally one. But Paul's Epistles and the Jerusalem Council (Acts 15) affirmed the validity of culturally distinct churches for culturally distinct peoples. The apostle Paul did not suffer from people-blindness as the Judaizers did.

The Judaizers, in fact, represented the most extreme form of the disease, that of cultural chauvinism. They felt that their Jewish culture was superior to, not just different from, that of the Gentiles. Of course, they tried to give good theological reasons as to why that was true, but they failed. There are no good theological reasons for suggesting that the way to eliminate group differences is for others to become "just like us." This kind of assimilationist philosophy had been quite common among Anglo-Americans up to the civil rights movements of the 1960s. Since then, however, the strong voices of minority groups have made us realize that the melting-pot theory may have constituted a kind of cultural chauvinism. The trend today is to recognize not only that black is beautiful, but that so also are all the other cultural subgroups in America. It is helping us get over our innate American tendencies toward people-blindness. It also may reduce our inclination to justify the American dream through quoting biblical proof texts.

Research into the way that churches grow has shown reasonably conclusively that evangelistic efforts based on the notion that all kinds of people should be encouraged to join the same local congregation are generally ineffective. Those who conduct such evangelism suffer from people-blindness. They are making a fundamental sociological error.

Sociological Tissue Rejection

People-blindness usually carries with it the inability to understand a very important human phenomenon which I like to describe as sociological tissue rejection. Medical science has discovered that blood transfusions and organ transplants from one body to another will be successful only to the degree that the types of blood or other tissue of the two persons involved match. If there is incompatibility between the organs, there will be rejection. For reasons that we do not fully understand, but which we nevertheless accept, God so made the human body that it prefers death to accepting foreign tissue, when that tissue is not a satisfactory match. This law of nature applies equally to believers and unbelievers. Conversion to Christianity does not allow a person with type A blood to receive a transfusion of type B blood and survive.

While we accept physical tissue rejection, we have a much more difficult time accepting the same phenomenon when applied to the social aspect of human life. It is a social fact, however, that some groups of people prefer the death or dissolution of their group to the alternative of accepting people whom they perceive as being incompatible. Something deeply inherent in human social psychology, whether in believers or unbelievers, tends to force them, consciously or unconsciously, to reject the foreign tissue.

Some Christian leaders spend a great deal of time trying to change this phenomenon. They might as well spend their time trying to make the Mississippi River flow north. Churches around the world and through history have grown basically among one kind of people at a time, and they show every indication that they will continue growing that way until the Lord returns.

Overcoming people-blindness is not simple. Blood types and Rh factors are easier to acknowledge than social types and their interrelationships. Whereas, for example, distinctions between Anglo-Americans and Afro-Americans and Hispanic-

Americans and Asian-Americans are quite simple to anyone with physical sight, that is only the beginning. The numerous subdivisions within each group are extremely important for church growth, but they are highly complex. The ability to discern and respect such divisions, I call people-vision.

Among Hispanic-Americans, for example, the differences between Cuban-Americans, Spanish-Americans, Puerto Ricans, and Mexican-Americans is important. But further, there are extremely important differences among Mexican-Americans themselves. Mexican-Americans in southern Texas are different from Mexican-Americans in northern New Mexico, and both groups are different from Chicanos in California's San Joaquin Valley. Some Mexican-Americans in Los Angeles, for example, speak mostly English in their homes, live in integrated neighborhoods, and may earn $25,000 per year. Other Mexican-Americans live in East Los Angeles *barrios*—they are undocumented, their youth belong to gangs, and their family income is often as low as $6,000 per year. While both groups are Los Angeles Mexican-Americans, they are vastly different from one another and in all probability cannot be folded into the same congregations, even if they become committed Christians.

Freedom in Rolling Hills

A very subtle group difference, this time among Anglo-Americans, was brought home to me when I once visited Rolling Hills Covenant Church. Rolling Hills is located south of Los Angeles on what is called the Peninsula. Housing is expensive, it is crisscrossed with bridle paths, and the residents are yacht and country club types. Rolling Hills Church is winning these people in large numbers, and it is growing fast. It may have the highest number of surgeons per capita of any church in the Los Angeles area.

While there, I had a long conversation with a surgeon's wife. She was vivacious, well-groomed, cultured, and an enthusiastic, active Christian. She felt that her spiritual gifts were being used in Rolling Hills Covenant Church and her Christian life was a joy. However, it had not always been that way. Previously, they had attended a small Baptist church where the members were also good Christians, evangelistically minded, friendly, and open to new people. But they were people of a lower socio-economic level, and try as they would, the women of that church simply did not know how to relate to this surgeon's wife. She felt frustrated. She tried to start Bible study classes, but they never seemed to get off the ground. She wondered if there might be something wrong with her spiritual life.

When she and her husband transferred to Rolling Hills Covenant, it was a different story. Without forcing anything, she could relate to the people on a peer level. She started Bible studies and they flew. For the first time, she felt she was being fulfilled in her Christian ministry.

The difference was not in the orthodoxy of the church or the friendliness of the people or in her own walk before the Lord. The difference was basically socio-cultural. Sociological tissue rejection was active, even though it was undetected. It was a difference that only those with people-vision could see, understand, and cope with.

Such social differences between groups of people must be kept in mind when churches plan evangelistic programs. They are crucial for both expansion growth (receiving new members into the present congregation), and for extension growth (starting new churches). If your evangelistic program has as its goal the folding of the new converts into your present congregation, take the time beforehand to understand the "group type" of your own church and the "group types" in your community. Then direct your initial efforts toward those neighborhoods and people who best match. This is the most effective way to go about E-1 evangelism.

If you decide to focus your evangelistic efforts on people of a different "group type," by definition, then, you are doing E-2 and E-3 evangelism. Do not use E-1 methods. The basic error of people-blindness is to try to do E-2 and E-3 evangelism with E-1 methods. One of the primary requirements of E-2 and E-3 evangelism is that new congregations must be started to receive the converts. And it must be expected from the beginning that the new congregations will differ from the mother church in various ways, some of which might be considered significant, and some trivial.

Death in the Nursery

A case of E-2 evangelism with results that were unanticipated because of people-blindness, occurred in two New Jersey cities, Franklin and Neptune. The Department of Church Extension of the Bible Fellowship Church had started new Bible Fellowship churches in both of these towns. Each one of the churches was around four years old when it died.

The Bible Fellowship Church is a small denomination of some 50 churches in Eastern Pennsylvania and New Jersey. They are an evangelistic sect and have been growing. Throughout their history they have established and maintained certain membership requirements that they feel are in accordance with the Scriptures. These concern some rules of behavior which are not agreed upon by all Christians, even by evangelical Christians who mutually accept the Bible as their ultimate authority for faith and practice.

I should mention in passing that such membership requirements usually are a sign of strength, not weakness, in a church. Dean Kelley's book, *Why Conservative Churches Are Growing,* has given a coherent sociological explanation as to why this is true. In relating this case, I am not suggesting that the Bible Fellowship Church, or any other church, should water down its membership requirements. I am simply showing how using E-1 methods for E-2 evangelism can kill churches.

As long as the new groups were "missions," there were few

59

problems. But when they began to mature and then applied for full membership in the denomination, on a par with the existing churches, some differences became evident. The families who had been won into the new churches in Franklin and Neptune happened to have a different cultural orientation from the traditional Bible Fellowship members. As frequently happens in cross-cultural situations, they studied the same Bible, but came to different conclusions as to how its teachings should be applied to contemporary life. Some of the particular areas that were called into question concerned divorce, tobacco, alcohol, and secret oath-bound societies. The issues were reminiscent of New Testament times, when eating meat offered to idols was discussed, and now, as then, there were at least two points of view.

When, after much negotiation and discussion, the issue came to a head, the Bible Fellowship Church decided they would maintain their strict requirements and not admit the new churches unless they conformed. The result was that both the young churches died a premature death. In retrospect, one might expect that the new churches would have been encouraged to continue, either as independent organizations, or as part of some denomination holding compatible views. But to suggest either of these options would have required an extraordinarily high degree of people-vision. Under the circumstances, the Bible Fellowship Church probably made the right decision, but it cannot expect to do much E-2 evangelism with that policy.[2]

Is This Discrimination?

Understanding the difference between E-1 evangelism and E-2/E-3 evangelism is not in any way to be confused with racism or discrimination. No church should be closed to receiving members from other racial or social groups who fulfill the membership requirements. Such a position has no place in the kingdom of God. Christians, because they have the love of the Holy Spirit in their hearts, can and do make the necessary adjustments to mix people from different groups, for the mutual enrichment of all concerned. But churches which major in doing this and build high-priority programs around it, most often find themselves losing evangelistic power and becoming increasingly irrelevant to the unbelievers of all the groups concerned.

It is much better to gather people from a certain social group into a congregation composed basically of people from that particular group. Once this is done, the resulting congregations should relate to one another with a spirit of love and interdependence, each with respect for the other's cultural integrity. The larger a local church is, the more such congregational subgroupings can occur within the total membership group. Usually, separate churches are necessary, however.

As a final illustration, Charles Mylander, one of the pastors of Rose Drive Friends Church in Orange County, California, did a study of a phenomenon he discovered operating between his church and the Yorba Linda Friends Church, only two miles away.[3] Here were two churches of the same denomination, both white Anglo-American congregations. The members lived generally in the same areas, both churches had lovely facilities, and both were growing well.

But the pastors of both churches gradually became aware that some people would show up at one church for a month or so and then disappear, only to be found later as full, active members of the other church. Mylander, who has good people-vision, went to work to discover why this was happening. He found that, while by most external criteria the churches seemed identical, they really were two distinct groups of people. The differences were subtle. They had to do with slight variations in educational levels, occupational roles, and housing choices. But these factors were strong enough that the people directly involved knew that for some reason they felt uncomfortable in one church, but at home in the

61

other. Without fully realizing it, they were looking for a church with "their kind of people."

In this case, the fact that there were two Friends churches instead of just one in that part of Orange County, increased the evangelistic potential of each of them. The members of both churches maintain good relationships, engage in some joint programs, and love one another in the Lord. Their distinctive personalities or "group types" are regarded by them as a strength, not a weakness.

The Cure for People-Blindness

The remedy for people-blindness is twofold: first theological, and then anthropological.

Theologically, moving from people-blindness to people-vision will require some deprogramming in many cases. The guilt feelings present in American social psychology as a result of centuries of racism and discrimination have been reflected in theologies. Some Christian theologians and ethicists have advocated an assimilationist stance toward groups in America, and have justified the melting pot in theological terms. Many American pastors were trained in seminaries which advocated assimilation, and it will take some theological rethinking to come to a position of respecting different cultural groups for what they are and of accepting their desire to maintain their own cultural identity and integrity. When this happens, the value of churches as authentic reflections of "their" culture, and not only of "ours," will be more and more appreciated.

Anthropologically, sensitivity to the significant components of culture and the way these can be recognized needs to be developed. Furthermore, anthropological insights help to reduce cultural chauvinism and allow people to recognize that while "our" culture might be *different* from "theirs," we need not assume that it is *better* than theirs. If this happens, tolerance will build respect for churches that might differ from ours with regard to the specific application and interpretation of biblical principles.

The net result of dispelling people-blindness will be an increased effectiveness in evangelistic efforts, as well as an increased harmony, understanding, and mutual interdependence among Christians of different races and social classes.

V.

Hyper-Cooperativism: Can Christian Unity Hinder Evangelism?

We live in an age when church cooperation, both formal and informal, is high. The World Council of Churches, founded in 1948, continues to thrive. The National Association of Evangelicals gains strength in America each year. Separatism, very strong during the thirties and forties, seems to have little appeal to the general evangelical public any more. Staunch denominational loyalty among church members seems to be at a low ebb; people nowadays look for more than denominational distinctives in a local church they are considering joining.

With cooperation the "in" thing these days, the danger of what we are calling hyper-cooperativism increases. I need to say here that this chapter in no way is intended to suggest that interchurch cooperation is a bad thing in itself. It is not in any way an anti-ecumenical polemic. I believe that we need more Christian brotherhood manifested in tangible ways, not less. But having said that, I will argue that cooperation among churches is more useful for accomplishing certain goals than for others.

Interchurch cooperation can be very useful for social action projects, for providing relief to victims of earthquakes or famines, for sponsoring theological seminaries, for promoting fraternal relationships between ministers, for programs of joint enrichment between churches of different cultures, for taking stands on certain political issues such as taxation of church properties, or even for projects involving E-2 or E-3 evangelism at home and abroad. But if the goal is evangelism that will result in church growth on the local level, the cooperative programs that have been tried to date have not proven to be very effective.

Church cooperation is a good thing. Hyper-cooperativism occurs when an attempt is made to use cooperation for the wrong ends. It can become counterproductive.

A False Premise

For at least a couple of decades, evangelicals, who have always been interested in effective evangelism and church growth, have been told that one way to evangelize more effectively is to cooperate interdenominationally on a local or regional level. Citywide evangelistic efforts have become popular and have constituted a prominent method of evangelization in America since the early fifties, and even before. Some nondenominational evangelistic agencies have come into being that have solicited resources both from the churches and from church members. Their promise, whether explicit or implied, has been that by supporting the citywide effort, more unbelievers will be won to Christ and folded into the churches, than without it. Some evangelists will refuse to come to a city unless a certain degree of interchurch support for the crusade is secured beforehand.

There has been little or no evidence that this premise is valid. In fact, research that has been done to date seems to indicate that just the opposite is true—the more churches cooperate interdenominationally in evangelistic projects, the less effectively they evangelize.

Of the several reasons why hyper-cooperativism reduces evangelistic effectiveness, perhaps the most important is that cooperative efforts tend to dilute the centrality of the local church. Citywide evangelistic efforts involving the churches of just one denomination are probably stronger than inter-denominational efforts, but the strongest of all is local church evangelism. In the typical citywide effort, the meetings are held in a neutral place, such as a stadium or a civic auditorium, and there is no natural connection between making a decision for Christ and commitment to a local church. Unless the local church remains central, evangelism that results in church growth will be minimal.

Positive Effects of Cooperative Evangelism

One's evaluation of the results of any evangelistic program will depend on the goals set for it. The assumption in this book, as in all church growth writings, is that evangelism should result in church growth. The biblical and theological reasons for this premise have been discussed at length elsewhere,[1] and do not need to be repeated. However, it must also be said that many citywide evangelistic efforts have brought positive results that cannot be measured in church growth. Some of them are as follows:

1. *E-0 evangelism.* In the previous chapter, we described E-1, E-2, and E-3 evangelism. E-0 evangelism is the last category in the series. It signifies the winning to Christ of a person who is already a church member, but who has never made a personal commitment to Christ. The latest statistics show that while 56 percent of American adults are active church members, only 30 percent are born-again Christians. That leaves some 26 percent who probably need E-0 evangelism.

When E-0 evangelism takes place, of course, the church does not grow visibly, because the person is already a member. But it becomes a better church. It grows in quality. And that is certainly a commendable thing.

2. *A rite of passage.* Anthropologists tell us that most societies have developed certain ceremonies which give visible public sanction to the milestone events in the life cycle of individuals. Big evangelistic crusades provide occasions for such rites of passage, both for the children of believers who need to express their faith publicly, and for others who have already made up their minds to become Christians and are looking for a good opportunity to do it. In all probability, both of these kinds of people would have done it anyway, but the citywide evangelistic crusade is as good an excuse as any.

3. *Public exposure to the gospel.* Citywide crusades tend to bring Jesus Christ to a high level of public attention. Television and radio spots, billboards, bumper stickers, large meetings written up in the papers, all help to draw public attention to the message. How much this actually aids in the total process of evangelization may vary according to the situation. Its effectiveness also depends on the previous level of awareness of the general public. In most cases, it can be listed as a positive benefit.

4. *Privatized Christians.* As Thomas Luckmann and other sociologists of religion have been pointing out, the phenomenon of privatized religion has been on the increase in America. While this involves religious expressions other than Christianity, undoubtedly an increasing number of Americans have been reconciled to God through Jesus Christ, but do not belong to a church, nor do they have any intention of joining one. Many undoubtedly are TV Christians. In their pajamas and slippers, they watch Rex Humbard or Oral Roberts or Robert Schuller or Jerry Falwell or others, while sipping coffee and munching a Danish pastry. They send contributions to these programs, and consider them their surrogate church.

Undoubtedly, many TV Christians are truly committed to Jesus Christ. They grow in their faith Sunday by Sunday. They read the Bible and pray with regularity. But the Church Growth Movement considers this an incomplete commitment. It teaches that a full commitment to Jesus Christ involves a simultaneous commitment to his body, the church. The Bible indicates that Christians are to relate to each other in the body of Christ (I Cor. 12), using their gifts to minister to one another.

Some, of course, are TV Christians by necessity. They are aged or disabled and could not go to church if they wanted to. But others are TV Christians by choice. While it is better to be a TV Christian than no Christian at all, I do not believe this should be encouraged as a substitute for responsible church membership.

E-0 evangelism, evangelistic rites of passage, increased public exposure to the gospel message, and privatized Christians are all positive results of cooperative evangelism. But none of them fully meets the expectations of average pastors who lead their churches into special evangelism programs. Deep down in their hearts, they want those programs to help their churches grow, through reaching unchurched men and women with the message of Christ and folding them into fellowship in their congregations. To the degree that this doesn't happen, they feel let down.

Biblically, the goal of the Great Commission is to make disciples. Making disciples is the only imperative verb in the Commission as found in Matthew:

> Go therefore and make diciples of all nations, baptizing them in the name of the Father and of the Son and of the Holy Spirit, teaching them to observe all that I have commanded you. (Matt. 28:19, 20 RSV)

Going, preaching, baptizing, teaching, and whatever else is necessary to make disciples—these are all important, but the final goal is to make disciples. With a rare exception or two, such as Joseph of Arimathea, biblical disciples were church members. They are described as continuing "stedfastly in the apostles' doctrine and fellowship, and in breaking of bread, and in prayers" (Acts 2:42). When authentic disciples are made, churches grow.

68

Evangelistic associations that report their final results in terms of attendance at crusades, decisions recorded, Bible studies joined, or anything less than responsible church membership, are fulfilling the Great Commission only partially. But the very nature of most cooperative evangelism, as we have seen, draws back from making church membership the bottom line against which to gauge their success or failure.

The Follow-up Gap

I began to understand some of the reasons for what I like to call the follow-up gap, when I made a study of the Evangelism in Depth program carried out in Latin America during the sixties. The follow-up gap is the difference between the number of persons who made recorded decisions during an evangelistic effort and those who become responsible church members.

Evangelism in Depth was the largest-scale attempt at cooperative evangelism in the history of Latin American Protestantism. It involved for an entire year all of the participating Protestant churches in each of ten republics. Behind it were some of the best evangelical minds, and the program was set up specifically to correct the follow-up gap discovered in crusade evangelism. But despite all the prayer and money and personnel invested, the follow-up gap was still there after the dust of the excitement had settled.

Hyper-cooperativism was by no means the only factor contributing to the lackluster showing of Evangelism in Depth. But it was one, and a significant one. It tended to reduce the message to the least common denominator. In one country, for example, the *Wordless Book* was banned from the children's program, because the committee chairperson disliked the red page that was designed to teach children about the blood of Christ. The program made an attempt to keep the focus sufficiently on the local church, but the total effect on church growth was disappointing.

Significantly, toward the end of the decade when disillusionment with Evangelism in Depth was surfacing, some denominations were severely criticized for refusing to enter the nationwide program when it came to their country. Their feeling that Evangelism in Depth would tend to retard their already vigorous growth patterns was not accepted. Some were accused of being divisive because they chose not to cooperate. But those denominations weathered the accusations and kept growing, because they felt they could evangelize better by doing their own thing in their own way.

Key 73 and Here's Life

Closer to home, the Key 73 program for nationwide evangelism in America was a disappointment to the majority of cooperating churches, largely due, in my view, to hyper-cooperativism. In this case, an inordinate amount of energy was demanded of church leaders across the board to accomplish the immense task of building bonds of interdenominational communication and cooperation. If ecumenism and cooperation had been the stated goals, Key 73 would have been a singular success. In fact, the *Christianity Today* editorial which sparked the entire movement hinted in its title, "Somehow, Let's Get Together," that perhaps cooperation might have been the first priority.

Evangelism, according to some analysts, entered the picture as a means to the end, which was cooperation. But the goal was interpreted to the average pastor in the pulpit as being evangelism, and most of them hoped against hope that Key 73 would be the program that would help their churches grow. When it didn't, they became disillusioned. What positive recollections they have now, five years later, usually relate to new friendships and improved Christian brotherhood, but not to accelerated church growth.

Not, I repeat, that there is anything wrong with cooperation between churches. It is a good thing in itself to bring together diverse members of the family of God from time to time. But the problem for church growth occurs when an evangelistic goal becomes replaced by an ecumenical goal.

An example of how this can happen was published in the *Here's Life America Southern California Communique* of November, 1976. The Here's Life America, or I Found It! movement constitutes the latest effort at nationwide cooperative evangelism in the U.S. One of the front-page items of this paper reported a meeting of 42 pastors who came together from divergent denominational backgrounds. They were uniting out of devotion to Jesus. They were making new friends and discovering a new way of life. But here is the joker. "They said the meeting alone was enough to make the entire Here's Life effort worthwhile."

Now I realize that I should not interpret this euphoric statement as I might a Bible text. Undoubtedly, if questioned further on this, of the 42 pastors involved, 42 would answer that their goal was evangelism, not ministerial fellowship. Certainly no one can question the evangelistic goal of Campus Crusade for Christ, the organizing agency. Nevertheless, the news item does serve to illustrate the danger of hyper-cooperativism.

The evangelistic results of Here's Life were somewhat disappointing. Of those who made decisions only 3 percent became church members.[2] Even adding to that number those persons who received E-0 evangelism and those who became TV Christians, there appears to be a rather large follow-up gap.

Perhaps one of the most institutionalized examples of hyper-cooperativism is the military chaplaincy. I have spoken with many chaplains who are evangelistic in outlook and who want their chapels to be effective centers for evangelism. Most of them are frustrated. Chapel growth on a military base is a very difficult thing to attain. The major reason for this might be a chronic case of hyper-cooperativism.

Protestant military chapels, according to regulations, have to be nondenominational. This is a distinct disadvantage. It is not possible under these rules for a chapel to develop a distinct philosophy of ministry geared specifically to the needs of a given target group. To suppose that military personnel constitute a homogeneous unit that could be naturally drawn together in one congregation is naive. The total ministry on a given base might be strengthened if the chaplains were encouraged to be more distinctive in their chapels, but this does not seem to be a possibility in the near future. Thus, success for most chaplains will have to be gauged in some terms other than chapel growth, given the present conditions which produce hyper-cooperativism.

Schaller on Cooperation

One of America's outstanding church diagnosticians, Lyle E. Schaller, has come to similar conclusions concerning hyper-cooperativism and church growth. He says,

> While this runs completely counter to the hopes and expectations of the advocates of church unity and intercongregational cooperation, the evidence is increasingly persuasive. Church growth and cooperative ministries are not compatible!

His five reasons, while admittedly speculative, bear examination and commentary as a summary to this chapter. To the degree they are understood, hyper-cooperativism can be avoided.

1. *"A cooperative ministry may blur the distinctive identity of each participating congregation."* This was seen in the case of the military chaplaincy. Churches with a well-understood philosophy of ministry have growth advantages over churches that continually have to ask themselves, "What are we here for, anyway?"

2. *"People unite with a specific worshiping congregation, not with a cooperative ministry."* There are some exceptions to this, as Schaller admits, but it is generally true. This is one reason why it is not helpful for church membership if the decision for

Christ is made in a place like a stadium, particularly in the midst of a week or two of meetings. The new Christian may attend several crusade rallies with their spotlights and crowds and 300-voice choirs and celebrities. It is a tough act for any local church to follow.

3. *"People with a strong interest in evangelism and church growth rarely are interested in interchurch cooperation and vice versa."* The exception to this would be the interdenominational evangelistic associations, which by their very nature depend on interchurch cooperation for the exercise of their ministry of evangelism.

4. *"Many cooperative ministries come into existence as the result of pressures of dwindling resources."* Church mergers, in particular, are often a clear sign of approaching decline, if not death. Church splits, hopefully intentional, are often signs of vitality and growth. Cell division, not cell fusion, produces healthy bodies.

5. *"Interchurch cooperation does use the time and energy of ministers and laity in creating and maintaining a new institution, and thus that time is not available for membership outreach."*[3] The broader the cooperation, the more complex the social relationships necessary to hold it together. Add to this the seemingly incompatible doctrines and policies, and the result is an association which is very demanding of available energy.

Is There Any Hope?

Because evangelism, which helps churches grow, and interchurch cooperation are both commendable activities, it seems reasonable to assume that there must be some way to join the two. Putting past disappointments to one side, it does appear now that some models for programs of cooperative evangelism, that in fact do result in measurable church growth, are emerging on the horizon.

Argentine evangelist Luis Palau and his team from Overseas Crusades have been pioneering what well may be a happy solution to the dilemma. The pilot project was the Rosario Plan, designed and executed in Rosario, Argentina, in 1975 and 1976. Over half of the Protestant churches in the city joined the movement, so it was a good example of interchurch cooperation. The difference was that, as early as 15 months before the Luis Palau crusade itself, teams of church growth experts, including Vergil Gerber, Juan Carlos Miranda, Edward Murphy, and Edgardo Silvoso, worked with the cooperating churches, helping each one to develop plans and goals for growth in its own congregation, as well as in new churches that they would plant.

Approximately 40 churches decided to cooperate. By the time Palau arrived, 45 *new* churches had been established. A strong growth process had been initiated, and converts were already being made at rates not seen in Rosario for years. The evangelistic event then was introduced into the growth process at the appropriate time. The barns were ready for the harvest, so to speak. Of the decisions registered during Palau's meetings, 57 percent were incorporated as members of churches.

The plan was tried again in Uruguay in 1978, and by the time Palau arrived, 140 new churches had been started there. At this writing, it is still too early to report the size of the follow-up gap.

The Process and the Event

As I see it, the secret of the success of the Rosario Plan, over community-wide efforts in other cities, is the skillful coordination of the evangelistic event with a growth process in the cooperating churches. When churches cooperating with interdenominational crusades are not in a healthy growth pattern themselves, the big meetings or the media blitz will not stimulate real growth. But when the church is already growing, and when it is in the habit of folding in new converts before the evangelistic event comes, the event can help the church grow. Two examples:

1. When Billy Graham held his crusade in Anaheim, California, in 1969, many Orange County churches had a pleasant, exciting experience, but little growth. The Garden Grove Community Church, already growing at a ten-year rate of over 500 percent, received hundreds of new members. It was ready for the harvest.

2. The national follow-up rate for Here's Life America was 3 percent. However, Lake Avenue Congregational Church in Pasadena, California, which had previously developed a sophisticated pattern of folding new converts under Pastor Kent Tucker, folded 30 of 74 decisions, a rate of 42 percent. The evangelistic event helped both churches, because it fit properly into an already established growth pattern.

My view is that, part and parcel of a great high-visibility evangelistic event sponsored by some interdenominational association, a long-range component of church growth planning and consultation should be provided. This needs to start one or two years before the event, and the timing of the event itself needs to remain flexible until all cooperating churches (or a predetermined percentage of them) have corrected the problems causing their nongrowth or slow growth and are reasonably sure that by the time of the event, they will be growing and absorbing new converts. When the cooperating churches are growing at a healthy rate, bring on the evangelist or the media blitz or whatever methodology may be appropriate. The follow-up gap will narrow dramatically, because the barns will be ready for the harvest.

This kind of thing can be done well through interchurch cooperation. Since the primary growth goals are not focused on the stadium, but on the local church, the local churches remain central to the program. And many local churches together can combine their resources to pay for area-wide media, the professional evangelist, and the church growth consultation services, which most local churches by themselves might not be able to afford.

In summary, then, cooperation is good, but hyper-cooperativism is not. In the past, cooperative efforts specifically for evangelism have not proved to be useful in helping cooperating churches to grow. Some more recent developments, however, seem to indicate that ways and means are being found to do cooperative evangelism without hyper-cooperativism, for the glory of God and the growth of his kingdom.

VI.

Koinonitis:
What Are Spiritual
Navel-Gazers?

Like hyper-cooperativism, koinonitis is a disease caused by too much of a good thing.

Koinonia is the biblical word for fellowship, a prominent Christian virtue. The Christians in that vigorous, healthy church in Jerusalem were characterized, among other things, by *koinonia* (Acts 2:42). The apostle Paul thanks God for the Philippian believers' *"fellowship* in the gospel" (Phil. 1:5). The apostle John says that Christians who walk in the light have *"fellowship* one with another" (I John 1:7).

Providing appropriate structures for fellowship to occur is essential for healthy church growth. When these are either nonexistent or when they become inoperative for some reason or other, the church fails to grow. Maladies which affect the fellowship dynamics of a church fall into the general category of koinonitis.

There are two areas in which koinonitis most frequently occurs. One could be said to involve the quality of the fellowship groups, and the other could be said to relate to their quantity. The first I might call fellowship inflammation and the second, fellowship saturation. Churches, whether large or small, which seem to have growth-inhibiting problems would do well to take a close look at both these areas.

A. Fellowship Inflammation

Everyone needs a certain amount of thyroid to maintain good physical health. But when something happens to the thyroid gland, other bodily systems are thrown off, and health is in jeopardy. *Koinonia* can easily be overdone until it becomes not just good Christian fellowship, but fellowship inflammation. The whole organism suffers.

Fellowship, by definition, involves interpersonal relationships. It happens when Christian believers get to know one another, to enjoy one another, and to care for one another. But as the disease develops, and *koinonia* becomes koinonitis, these interpersonal relationships become so deep and so mutually absorbing, they can provide the focal point for almost all church activity and involvement. Church activities and relationships become centripetal.

It is easy to understand how this happens. It takes time and effort and energy to establish friendly relationships with others and to nourish them to the point where fellowship is occurring. Each person in a fellowship group has a considerable investment in the social dynamics there. When the investment pays off, and the relationships become established, a protective mechanism begins to build. Both clergy and laity may find themselves spending most of their church time enjoying each other. Before they know it, the group can degenerate into a circle of spiritual navel-gazers. Everyone involved feels so good about everyone else, that often the disease is not noticed. It is one of those silent, almost symptomless diseases, something like high blood pressure in the human. If constant measurements are not taken, the problem can increase until it is too late to correct it.

Evangelistic Myopia

Churches with acute fellowship inflammation do not grow. This is the end result of koinonitis, although the cause and effect are often hidden to those who are enjoying the fellowship. In fact, in extreme cases, churches with koinonitis don't care whether they grow or not.

The reason for this is that somewhere in the process of developing the disease, the focus on the church's philosophy becomes "us." The church exists for itself and its members and not for those who are outside the fellowship. The people within the church have been reconciled to God, and they love each other. Who cares about those outside? Bible verses mentioning that some people are lost, or that God is not willing that any should perish, or that Christians are supposed to preach the gospel to every creature are not stressed.

Usually it is unintended, but an evangelistic myopia develops as a symptom of koinonitis. Lost men and women are out there all around, but no one in the church can see them, so to speak. The importance is placed on the people who are saved, not on those who are unsaved. Some churches with evangelistic myopia develop an aversion to anything that smacks of sharing the gospel. Soul-winning is considered almost abnormal Christian behavior. Why win other people to Christ? They would disturb our fellowship!

Church growth? It is even more threatening than evangelism to those with koinonitis. I recently saw an article in a prominent Christian magazine hinting that church growth could be a heretical position. The article argued that "small is beautiful," and warned churches against becoming victims of growth. Instead of quoting Jesus' command to "Go . . . and make disciples of all nations" (Matt. 28:19 RSV), the article emphasized Jesus' statement that "Where two or three are gathered in my name, there am I in the midst of them" (Matt. 18:20 RSV).

Few Christians would admit they have evangelistic myopia. Christians know they are supposed to have a concern for the lost, a "passion for souls." Even the article I mentioned properly tips its hat to the church as an agency for proclaiming the gospel. But somehow that proclamation is not supposed to result in new men and women being reconciled to God,

79

coming into the fellowship, and thereby helping the church to grow. It is often said, "We are interested in quality, not quantity." The quality of that church in Jerusalem which was enjoying fellowship (Acts 2:42), but to which the Lord was also adding "daily such as should be saved" (Acts 2:47), is apparently not the sort of quality that those with evangelistic myopia value highly. That quality makes churches grow.

The Sanctification Gap

Koinonitis often carries with it a high degree of piety, and it opens what might be called a sanctification gap. This creates an excessive distance between those within the church and those outside the church.

The sanctification gap presents a dilemma, because piety and sanctification are normal results of the process of Christian growth. We are all to become more Christlike. The Christian life-style is not to be "conformed to this world," but "transformed," we are told in Romans 12:2. Worldly habits are to drop out of a Christian's life, as dead leaves fall off a tree when new life surges through in the springtime.

While Christian behavior patterns are supposed to be distinct from the world's behavior, Christians are still required to keep contact with non-Christian people, communicate the gospel to them, and fold those who accept the gospel into fellowship. The first is often simple; folding them into the fellowship is something else again. In churches with koinonitis, the new Christian feels about as comfortable as a teen-ager in a nursing home. A short visit is OK, but the residents of a nursing home would be unlikely to invite teen-agers to move in. One experience of rock music on the stereo until midnight would tend to wear their welcome very thin.

This is analagous to the problem of churches which have developed a sanctification gap. Since the members are all mature Christians, their tolerance level for the behavior of new and immature Christians may be quite low. Although the older Christians do all they can to prevent it, their attitudes are telegraphed in a number of ways to the new believers, and before they know it, the newcomers have evaporated.

How can the sanctification gap be prevented? Certainly not by advocating that Christians become more worldly. The way to close the gap is to structure the fellowship in such a way that it includes Christians of all stages of maturity. Room must be made for what the Bible calls "babes in Christ." If koinonitis continues, this is impossible to do, because it is too disturbing to the established fellowship patterns.

If those of us who are parents recall that time when new babies came into our homes, we will get an idea of the effect new Christians might have on a church. New babies in the home are a terrible nuisance. They yell and scream at all hours of the day and night. They show no respect for their elders. They dirty their diapers and demand to be changed. They insist on eating, and then sometimes throw up their food. They can't be left alone, so they sharply curtail their parents' mobility. They cost money and make no economic contributions. They don't even understand what you're saying. But despite these negative qualities, you love them, you're glad they're there, you wouldn't trade them for anything in the world—and you're also very glad when they grow up.

The Lord knew that my wife and I possessed only enough parental energy to go through that experience three times. Our three girls are now growing up, and we are looking forward to the day when they will all be well-situated in their own homes and careers. We feel that we can live the rest of our lives with no more babies in the house, except perhaps for the occasional visit of a grandchild or two. If we were a church instead of a family, we would have koinonitis.

Church fellowship groups cannot afford to develop the feeling toward new Christians that my wife and I have toward new babies. There must always be some of them around. Their behavior patterns must be accepted. Just as babies are not born mature, neither are born-again people mature when first delivered. They will grow up and develop piety and sanctification such as the older ones have, but it will take time. Meanwhile, they need to feel loved and wanted. They need to know there are no price tags on the acceptance by the group. When they fall, they need to be picked up and coddled until they are ready to try again.

If these suggestions are put into practice, the sanctification gap will disappear. When a new Christian comes into the church, he or she will find many others to identify with. In a growth situation, new Christians abound, and koinonitis will usually no longer be a problem.

When I studied the Pentecostals in Latin America some years ago, I found they had a workable system for avoiding the sanctification gap. One of the chief ways they make contact with new people is through open-air meetings on street corners and in the plazas. In one church in Chile, for example, when people receive Christ as their Savior, they are required to appear in an open-air service the next Sunday and give their testimonies in public. Sanctification usually has had little chance to operate in their lives, and the unchurched people can identify with the way the new converts tell their stories. Their unpolished delivery and unrefined vocabulary make good sense to those who hear them. In that church, one can always find Christians in all stages of development, and this is one reason why it has been able to grow to 80,000 members—as far as I know, the largest church in the world.[1]

Where Koinonitis Flourishes

Although any church may develop koinonitis, there are three groups in particular in which it needs to be recognized as a special danger area. These are the charismatic movement, the church renewal movement, and strongly group-conscious churches.

The charismatic movement has brought fresh winds of the Spirit to many a decrepit church and enabled it to catch fire for God once again. It has been a wonderful thing for hundreds of thousands of American Christians, and through the new vitality of the charismatic movement, large numbers of people have been born again. I have no question in my mind about the outstanding evangelistic vision and ministry of the charismatic movement.

However, charismatic groups need to watch out for koinonitis. This paragraph I saw some time ago illustrates my meaning:

> A number of leaders are expressing concern that the main guiding forces of the charismatic movement seem to emphasize discipleship, teaching, and community at the expense of evangelism as a top priority. These leaders see a specter of stagnation hovering over the scene.[2]

If the charismatic movement is to remain a vital instrument for the Holy Spirit in today's world, it must avoid this eventuality at all costs.

The church renewal movement has been used by God in a beautiful way during the past couple of decades. Many churches that had been stuck on dead center for years have come to life through the ministry of those associated with the church renewal movement. A great deal of E-0 evangelism has been accomplished. People have established close relationships with Jesus Christ, and with one another.

But the church renewal movement has not distinguished itself in consistent and effective evangelistic outreach programs in the renewed churches. Some groups have done it well, but others may have developed koinonitis. Small-group experiences play a prominent part in much church renewal, and these are the groups that need to avoid the disease. When fellowship becomes too close, in fact, other dangers arise. Some reports have it that among certain leaders of the church renewal movement and in certain churches that have experienced a great degree of group fellowship, a higher than average divorce rate has developed. This result, like other side effects of koinonitis, needs to be guarded against.

83

Dangers of Group Consciousness

Some churches by nature have a higher group consciousness than others. Moravians and Mennonites and some
Reformed churches are examples of churches with high group
consciousness. Methodists, Episcopalians, and United Presbyterians have a much lower group consciousness. It is a sign
of high group consciousness when church rolls have certain
surnames that seem to be repeated frequently—intermarriage
has tended to perpetuate the group.

A church with a high group consciousness has more of a
tendency toward koinonitis than do other churches. The
Seventh-day Adventists, for example, have a high group
consciousness. The danger of their contracting koinonitis has
been recognized by Gottfried Oosterwal, a professor at
Andrews University. In his book on church growth among
Seventh-day Adventists, he says this factor hinders growth in
many an Adventist congregation: "New members, without an
Adventist background, often do not feel at home in the
church."

He explains that outsiders do not naturally share the
"Adventist group experience," they do not know "Adventist
language," and Adventist behavior seems strange to them.
Seventh-day Adventists themselves are somewhat counterculture. They worship on a different day, they eat different
foods, they have different standards of dress than most
Anglo-Americans. This is a denominational strength which
both they and outsiders fully recognize. Oosterwal argues,

All this would not be so bad—for it points to the strength of the
church as a group-religion and a whole way of life—were it not
for the fact that the other members of the church, reared in an
Adventist community and usually unaware of the struggle of the
new members, *offer them no help in this matter*.

He found that all rapidly growing Adventist churches have
solved this problem and have become open and helpful to new

members. He doesn't use the word, but the growing churches have recovered from koinonitis.[3]

Some churches have developed around extended families and these, too, need to be aware of the dangers of koinonitis. I have a report, for example, that in the First Christian Church of Harriman, Tennessee, out of 250 members, only 5 were not related to the others by blood or marriage. That was some years ago, and the church is now dead. Koinonitis is not necessarily terminal, but it can kill if it goes too far.

B. Fellowship Saturation

If fellowship *inflammation* and all its ramifications have to do with the *manner* in which people relate to each other, fellowship *saturation* has to do with the *number* of people who relate to each other.

In order to understand this kind of koinonitis, it is necessary to understand the three basic internal structures of a church. I have called these three structures the internal organs of the body of Christ. They are the celebration, the congregation, and the cell.

The celebration is the membership group of the church. It usually meets on Sunday morning for worship, but it may meet also at other times. If you belong to a church, you are de facto part of the celebration.

The congregation is a fellowship group. A church may have just one, or it may have many. This is a group in which all the members know one another. Although there is no limit on the size of the celebration, the congregation ideally should have between 40 and 120 members.

The cell is the spiritual kinship group. In it, the members not only know one another, they share their lives with one another on a deeper level. Interpersonal relationships are more intimate in the cell than in the congregation. Cell members make themselves spiritually accountable to one another. Its ideal size is 8 to 12 members.

Folding new members into the church usually takes place in the congregation or in the celebration. Some churches also use cells for folding, but if so, they are specifically designed as "reproductive" cells, rather than "nutritive" cells. Reproductive cells need to be specifically structured to prevent koinonitis.

Koinonitis is usually not a severe growth problem in either the celebration or the cell. But in that intermediate grouping called the congregation, koinonitis can easily occur, not only through the ways that have been described as fellowship inflammation, but also by becoming too large. Congregations which approach the 120 mark are susceptible to fellowship saturation. Congregations which are larger than 120 are in trouble and will probably begin to plateau.

The reason for this is directly related to the function of the group. While fellowship groups can take several different forms, such as adult Sunday school classes, task-oriented groups, neighborhood groupings, or others, the function is the same: to provide social fellowship one with another.

Research has found that the average church member knows 40 to 60 other people in the church on a first name basis, no matter whether the church has 100, 500, or 5,000 members. Part of the function of a congregation is for each member to know all the others. In a group of up to 60 members, it can be done very well. With more than 60, it begins to stretch. At 120, the average person will know only one out of every two people, and the fellowship function is greatly diminished. Before this happens, attitudes may have developed which tend to exclude outsiders. Outsiders are not excluded because they might be incompatible with current members; they are excluded because the fellowship function is already saturated and operating at very low efficiency.

Note that fellowship saturation occurs in both small and large churches. Smaller churches may have only one fellowship group. If so, and if the fellowship group does not divide, the church itself will not grow to many more than 120 active adult members. It might get up to 200 and then plateau. This is one reason why a full 80 percent of American churches have 200 or fewer in worship attendance.

But in larger churches which have many fellowship groups, this kind of koinonitis may constitute a practically invisible barrier to growth. Fellowship groups or congregations should be identified and examined. If koinonitis has become a problem for any of them, it needs to be dealt with, if the church is going to regain health.

Getting Over Koinonitis

The cure for koinonitis is fairly simple: divide. If fellowship inflammation is the problem, the fellowship groups should be broken up, if for nothing else than just to disturb the status quo and force some new alignments. When this happens, conscious steps need to be taken to be sure the resulting groups are open to outsiders and that newcomers are properly cared for. The best way to do this is to incorporate newcomers, preferably new Christians, as soon as possible.

If fellowship saturation is the problem, the growing congregation should plan to divide when the membership approaches 100. Two new groups of 50 each are large enough to provide social fellowship, but small enough to avoid koinonitis. This kind of division should constitute a pattern. It should be a regular part of the church's life-style.

Now, I know that the cure for koinonitis is not easy. *Koinonia* is a precious thing, and dividing groups invariably means breaking up fellowship. However, I can think of many cures for human diseases which are not pleasant but which we undergo in order to be healthy again. Church groups should have the same attitude. Groups need to divide, not for convenience, but for growth. Those who take seriously the commands of our Lord to "make disciples of all nations" will be glad to pay that price and receive God's blessing in renewed growth.

VII.

Sociological Strangulation: Can Good Growth Be Choked Off?

Of the eight diseases identified and described in this book, only one—sociological strangulation—is a disease of a growing church. Growing churches that wish to maintain their growth rate need to watch out for it. Sociological strangulation can usually be predicted up to five years in advance, although few churches have the foresight and courage to act on their knowledge in time.

The term itself, "sociological strangulation," is not a new one. Other writers, notably Richard Meyers, have been using it for some time. The expression may not contain the most felicitous choice of words, but like names of many human diseases, if it is used regularly, it simply becomes part of one's vocabulary. After all, "spinal meningitis" is not an easy term to learn, but we use it. The concept behind sociological strangulation certainly is valid, and I see no reason to suggest that the terminology be changed.

Potbound Churches

What is sociological strangulation? It is the slow-down in the rate of church growth caused when the flow of people into a church begins to exceed the capacity of the facilities to handle it. In other words a church, like a plant, can become "potbound." If the root system gets too big for the pot, the plant will grow less and, as Japanese gardeners know, what growth there is may turn out to be grotesque. This is an interesting diversion for gardeners, but not for churches. Healthy, vigorous church growth requires space.

Growing churches that wish to continue to grow need to be very much aware of this danger. As we have said, it can be predicted, and with proper planning it can be avoided. If plans are not made, and if the growth momentum falls victim to sociological strangulation, the growth process can come to a fairly abrupt halt. If and when that happens, it is much more difficult to regain the lost momentum that it would have been to prevent the difficulty before it occurred.

The reasons special courage is needed to deal with sociological strangulation are that (a) facility needs cannot be handled immediately, and (b) usually a substantial budgetary allocation, and perhaps a special fund drive, are necessary to care for the situation. Very few congregations can be motivated to take vigorous budgetary action unless an emergency is at hand. The purpose of the kind of planning I am suggesting is to *avoid* an emergency, but that is not always easy to communicate. Blessed is the church that has the leadership capable of motivating preventive action, rather than just therapeutic action.

There are two particular danger areas in which sociological strangulation is known to affect the growth of a church—parking area and sanctuary space. Other facility needs, such as Christian education rooms, space for social activities, administrative offices, and music rooms are also important. But there is little question in the minds of church planners that parking and sanctuary considerations must take top priority. Let's consider them one at a time.

Parking

The church growth specialist who has best expressed this first need is Robert Schuller in his book, *Your Church Has Real*

Possibilities.[1] In it he has a fascinating chapter entitled "Seven Principles of Successful Retailing." While many theologians have been decrying the use of Madison Avenue techniques in the church, Robert Schuller has the audacity to come right out and say that churches are really in the business of retailing religion. I want to be the first to agree with both sides. There certainly are many manipulative features of Madison Avenue advertising that should not be adopted by Christians. But on the other hand, it makes a great deal of common sense to understand churches as analagous to retailers. Interpreting God's will and his kingdom to the general public is the task of the local church. As a Christian friend of mine who is in the advertising business says, "Sell it like it is."

Schuller's principle of successful retailing that relates to sociological strangulation is "surplus parking." Understanding the importance of this is, in America, basically a cultural matter. Lack of parking is not a deterrent to church growth among the Danis of Irian Jaya or the fishermen of Bangladesh. But contemporary America has made the use of the automobile a central cultural value. Whether it *ought* to be that way or not makes a good topic for a debating society or for Christian social ethicists. But until they decide it to the satisfaction of all, the fact remains that large numbers of American people, whom our churches are responsible for winning to Jesus Christ, do consider their automobiles an essential part of their life-styles. Wheels are classified as a necessity of life, along with food, clothing, and housing.

Of course, there are some exceptions. Automobiles can be considered a handicap on Manhattan Island, for example. But there are very few areas across the country where this would be true. Most Americans use their cars when they have to go even three or four blocks to buy a newspaper or pick up a child. Americans use their cars for grocery shopping, for transportation to work, to go out for an evening, or to visit friends. Successful shopping centers, athletic stadiums, libraries, colleges, and amusement parks all plan far in advance for surplus parking. They have learned that when the average American finds a parking lot full, or so nearly full that it is difficult to find a place to park, he or she is not likely to return to that place very frequently. This is an important lesson for churches as well.

There ought to be empty parking spaces in the church parking lot during the peak traffic moments at the Sunday morning worship services. If the parking lot is full at that time, the church will usually have sociological strangulation. It is a sign that evangelistic effectiveness probably has begun to diminish. In most cases, faithful members and Christian workers are accustomed to getting to church early, and they take the choice spaces in the parking lot. Furthermore, they often occupy that space from the beginning of the Sunday morning activities until the end, even when there are multiple services.

Strangers and visitors usually arrive about five minutes before the worship service starts. If they find the parking lot full, and if they have to drive around the streets, and if they have to walk some distance to get from their car to the church, and if they arrive late for the worship service, the whole experience might prove too much for them. They may not be in the mood to appreciate even the best of worship services, choir presentations, or biblical messages. Some may go elsewhere next Sunday. Others even may decide that they can find something better to do than go to church on Sunday morning, if it involves that much hassle.

It is one thing to respond to this behavior by saying, "If that is their attitude, good riddance." It is another to say, "God loves these people and so do we. It is our job to attract them to the Savior, not turn them away."

Solving the Parking Problem

As far as I know, there are two major ways to solve the sociological strangulation caused by inadequate parking. One is to buy new land, and the other is to park at a distance.

The most obvious solution to the problem is to purchase adjoining land and expand the parking facilities to accommodate those who want to use it. City zoning ordinances usually require the provision of adequate parking when new facilities are built. But if present facilities are already overcrowded, it will soon show up in parking. A problem for many urban churches is the inflated value of real estate in the immediate vicinity of the church. Many churches made their first property purchase at $5 to 10 thousand per acre, only to be faced with $50 to 100 thousand per acre for additional parking. This is one reason many churches purchasing new sanctuary sites now are looking for 15 to 20 acres to begin with. The cost of multiple-level parking garages has been found almost universally prohibitive.

An alternative way to deal with the problem of inadequate parking is to require, to the extent possible, that church members leave home early and park at a distance from the church. Some can find curbside parking several blocks away from the church and walk in. The Sunday morning use of nearby off-street parking lots can often be negotiated with businesses, shopping centers, or restaurants in the vicinity. If these parking lots are distant, shuttle-bus services can be set up to transport members to and from the church campus.

It is not always easy to convince members that they should do this, and once begun, it is not always easy to enforce. There has to be a high degree of *esprit de corps* among the members, and it has to be seen as a substantial contribution to the mission of the church, and to church growth. A couple of years ago, for example, our pastor announced that members of our church were to park at a distance, in order to leave ample parking for the elderly, handicapped, marginal attenders, and visitors. Some did for a while, but there has been no pastoral pressure to keep it up, and I am amazed at how many faithful members unashamedly take up space in the parking lot during peak times on Sunday mornings. They are contributing to acute sociological strangulation, but most of them do not realize it. If they did, they would resume leaving home fifteen minutes early and walking four or five blocks to church.

Just how many churches have successfully operated shuttle-bus service from distant parking lots, I do not know. I have seen it operating, for example, in Grace Community Church of the Valley in Panorama City, California. Another church doing it well is Los Gatos Christian Church in Los Gatos, California. In a recent church bulletin, Pastor Marvin Rickard wrote,

> We have grown steadily in the four years here, and others come each Sunday. Traffic congestion is actually less now than when we moved in, although attendance is double. The reason, of course, is our Park and Ride bus service, now a way of life for hundreds each week.

Seventeen hundred use the shuttle buses each Sunday, according to the latest figures I have. It can be done, with constant encouragement and a motivation to contribute to church growth.

The Sanctuary

The seating capacity of the sanctuary is the second danger area, perhaps even more acute than lack of parking. As a rule of thumb, when the sanctuary is 80 percent full and the church is growing, you can expect that sociological strangulation has already begun to set in. Growth rates will almost invariably begin to drop at that point. If the church is otherwise healthy, it might keep on growing as the 80 percent point is passed, but the annual rate will usually become slower and slower.

There are exceptions to this, of course. Some churches which have developed extremely powerful growth dynamics will surpass the 80 percent and even the 100 percent mark. Until the fire inspector puts a stop to it, some churches can provide seating with extra chairs in the aisles, seats on stairways, and even on the floor. Others can utilize overflow auditoriums with closed circuit television. But these should be seen as temporary measures at best. Such auxiliary provisions will soon be at capacity themselves, and growth will be choked off.

As I see it, there are three major long-term options for curing this kind of sociological strangulation. Depending on the local circumstances, one of the three should probably become part of the church planning, well before attendance in the present sanctuary reaches the 80 percent capacity level.

Add Another Service

The first, and often the most economical option is to add another Sunday worship service. Going from one service to two immediately doubles the seating capacity of the sanctuary. Several secondary considerations need to be planned for, when considering multiple services. For example, the timing must insure that the parking lot can be emptied between services. Also, in many churches, the Sunday school classes must be smoothly coordinated with the worship services, so neither obstructs the growth of the other.

One church making the maximum use of multiple services is the Church on the Way in Van Nuys, California. Their sanctuary seats only 450, but with overflow seating and multiple services, they are handling a weekly attendance of 3,000. They now run five identical Sunday services, three in the morning and two in the evening.

Many churches can successfully go from one to two worship services on a Sunday morning, but others cannot. The difference depends largely on the particular philosophy of ministry of the church. Some worship styles virtually rule out the possibility of duplicate services. Generally speaking, a worship format which requires a high level of emotional output on the part of the preacher cannot easily be duplicated. Perhaps the majority of black churches and southern white pentecostal churches, for example, would find themselves in this position. In churches like these, where there is a strong vocal audience response to what the preacher says, the energy output of both preacher and congregation is enormous. By the time most of these preachers finish their sermons, they are drained, both physically and emotionally. Typically, they are no more capable of repeating the effort than a professional basketball team is capable of playing a doubleheader.

However, other philosophies of ministry demand an energy output more analagous to a baseball game. Baseball players, with the exception of the pitcher, and sometimes the catcher, are able to play doubleheaders. The energy output is considerably lower than in basketball.

Most non-pentecostal Anglo-American preachers have been trained to use large amounts of their energy during the week while preparing their Sunday sermons. By the time they enter the pulpit, they are ready to speak from extended notes or a manuscript or even from rote memory. Some of them, nevertheless, preach with a good deal of expression and movement, but compared to black and southern pentecostal preachers, the energy level is minimal. If one uses good principles of larynx control so the voice doesn't tire, this kind of preaching can be repeated two or three times on a Sunday morning and can be expected to have a similar effect on the congregation each time.

The more sedate and liturgical a church's worship services are, then, the more possibility it has for solving sociological strangulation by going to multiple services.

It may occur to some churches that a variation of this option would be to have different staff members preach at different Sunday morning services. There are some places where this is being done with good results. However, such cases are unusual. Unless a church has a very special growth mix that will permit this to happen and still allow the church membership to increase, it should not be regarded as a very significant possibility. The pastor of the church is the key to its growth, and his major role is to provide leadership for the congregation. This leadership is usually projected in a uniquely important way through the Sunday sermon. For this reason, church growth pastors will not relinquish the pulpit readily.

Build a Larger Sanctuary

The second option for solving the problem of sanctuary capacity is to build a larger one. This, of course, is expensive. The larger the church, the more expensive. At this writing, for example, the Garden Grove Community Church in Garden Grove, California, is suffering from sociological strangulation. The sanctuary capacity is slightly under 2,000 and worship attendance is around 7,000. Pastor Robert Schuller conducts two identical services, and an earlier, but less popular, service is led by another staff member. Extra seating is provided by a drive-in parking lot, allowing worshipers to remain in their cars, and by setting up folding chairs out on the lawn. But because of inadequate sanctuary capacity, the growth rate of the church has been dropping off during the past few years. It was growing between 300 and 500 percent per decade, but the rate now is down to 46 percent.

As a solution to this problem, the church has broken ground for a new sanctuary, providing inside seating for 4,100, plus 1,500 automobiles in the drive-in parking lot. My guess is that when the new sanctuary is opened, the growth rate will go up to around 300 percent per decade again. In the case of Garden Grove, because of its unusual "crystal cathedral" architectural design, the price tag is around $15 million, much higher than most churches might be willing to go.

However, multimillion-dollar sanctuaries are not as unusual now in the seventies as they have been in the past. The Huffman Assemblies of God in Birmingham, Alabama, for example, is building a church to seat 10,000, which I believe will be the largest in the United States. In the southern part of California alone, not counting Garden Grove, I am aware of five churches seating between 2,500 and 4,000, all built within the last five years. A national survey would undoubtedly reveal many more.

Even announcing plans for a new sanctuary can often cause enough excitement, anticipation, and hope to turn a decreasing growth rate around. One of the world's largest churches, the Full Gospel Central Church of Seoul, Korea, found it had sociological strangulation when its membership reached 8,000, while its sanctuary seated only 2,000. The growth rate had dropped to only 27 percent per decade in the late sixties. Then in 1970, the church decided to build a sanctuary seating 10,000, and from 1970 to 1973 the rate went up to 308 percent per decade. When the $5 million building was dedicated and put to use, the rate went up to an amazing 1,155 percent per decade. At this writing the membership has passed the 50,000 mark, and plans have been announced for yet another sanctuary in a different part of the city which will seat 30,000. To my knowledge, this will be the largest sanctuary in the world, the second largest being the Brazil for Christ Church in Sao Paulo, which seats 25,000.

New sanctuary construction is one option, but not the only one, for curing sociological strangulation. Before a church decides to go this route, it is often wise to employ a knowledgeable church growth consultant to examine the dynamics and the advisability of investing in a new sanctuary.

Agree on an Optimum Expansion Size

The third option for action when sociological strangulation approaches is to agree on an optimum size for the church, and plan not to grow by expansion growth any further. Before the church reaches the optimum size, begin spinning off groups of members who will start new churches in the area. That will keep present facilities adequate for membership, and it will also continue to stimulate the total growth process.

Redwood Chapel in Castro Valley, California, has been

doing this for some years, under the dynamic leadership of Pastor Sherman Williams. With a sanctuary seating 650 and two Sunday services, the church has set an optimum membership level of 900. Over the past few years, hundreds of members have volunteered to spin off and provide the nucleus groups for new churches in the area.

The use of house churches is also catching on in some places. Howard Snyder's book, *The Problem of Wineskins*, has been a contributing influence in the planning of at least two growing churches in my own area. One of these is the Church on the Way in Van Nuys. It has already been mentioned that Pastor Jack Hayford preaches five identical services each Sunday. But he has also organized nearly 200 home worship groups, each conducting a Sunday worship service once a month. Every member of the church is expected to belong to a home group and worship away from the church one Sunday per month. This in itself reduces the people flow at the mother church by 25 percent. When they go to two home worship services per month, it will reduce it by 50 percent. Pastor Hayford hopes to establish 2,500 of these groups over the next few years and thereby handle a total membership of 50,000.

Another person who is using home churches to good advantage is Pastor Robert Hymers of the Open Door Community Churches. For three years he has been laying the foundation for a church system that conducts all its Sunday morning worship services in homes. He now has seven house churches functioning among such diverse groups as Hispanic-Americans, Jews, Catholics, and Anglo-Americans. The growth rate was 77 percent last year, and almost all of that was conversion growth. On Sunday evenings, all the members of all the house churches come together in a rented facility, where they have a celebration with Pastor Hymers preaching and nurturing the flock.

Hymers' goal is to double the number of house churches each year, until they reach 1,000 groups. At the current average of 35 persons per group, the total membership would then be 35,000. And all this with no sanctuary or building program of their own!

Combining the Three

The three options for curing sociological strangulation are obviously not mutually exclusive. My own church, Lake Avenue Congregational Church, has had the problem for some time, and is trying all three remedies simultaneously.

The sanctuary seats 1100, and for some time now Pastor Raymond Ortlund has been preaching three services. The church has sociological strangulation, and the growth rate has been dropping. The church recently went through a process of long-range planning and decided to take two bold steps in order to maximize the potential of reaching new people in its immediate area, the San Gabriel Valley. The first concerns the new sanctuary and parking, and the second consists of starting new churches.

The church felt that it should keep growing on the present campus. By the providence of God, one of the new freeways in the area was constructed immediately along the southern property line of the church campus. Not only that, but the main interchange for the city of Pasadena was constructed on Lake Avenue, giving the church excellent visibility and accessibility. So a decision was taken to build a new sanctuary which will seat 3,000. Two services on Sunday morning will be the norm, which means that with the new sanctuary, the church can grow from the present 3,000 to 6,000 by 1990. The goal is to reach 3,000 new people by expanding the facilities.

But at the same time the facilities are being expanded, the church has decided to challenge its members to start 10 new churches in the San Gabriel Valley by 1990, each of them having a membership of between 1,000 and 1,500. At this writing a nucleus of 60 has been formed for the first daughter church. On October 22, 1978, it was commissioned and sent off with a newly ordained pastor. Through new churches, if God

99

blesses, between 10,000 and 15,000 people will eventually be reached for Christ. The projected result will be a family of churches, not just one church, and the total number of new people will be three or four times as many as could be handled, if the only solution adopted had been to expand the present campus.

Sociological strangulation can usually be avoided by careful long-range planning. The first step is to be aware that it exists and to recognize its symptoms as early as possible.

VIII.

Arrested Spiritual Development: Why Don't You Act Your Age?

Human beings whose growth is retarded are often victims of arrested physical development. A gland or a digestive malfunction or nerve damage might cause this. A recent news item told of an extreme case of child abuse, in which a seven-year-old girl was discovered in a small closet where her parents had kept her all her life. She couldn't walk, she had learned to say only a few words, and she weighed under 40 pounds. Hers was a pathetic case of arrested physical development. She probably will never be normal.

The causes for nongrowth in many churches can be traced to spiritual conditions which are parallel to that kind of arrested physical development. When people in the church are not growing in the things of God or in their relationships with one another, the total health of the church deteriorates, and the church cannot grow.

Arrested spiritual development is a problem connected with internal growth, sometimes referred to as "quality growth." If a survey were taken, this might turn out to be the most prevalent growth-obstructing disease in American churches. A church that is just barely limping along, carrying out a program, raising a budget, hiring a preacher, holding worship services, and doing whatever else churches are "supposed" to do, is just "playing church." Merely going through the motions is not a ministry that makes a significant impact on a community. But, unfortunately, it does describe many churches in America.

Arrested spiritual development is definitely a curable disease. The first step toward therapy is to understand the problem and some of its ramifications. Once it is understood, there are ways and means of correcting the problems through biblical teaching, the guidance of other Christians, and the leadership of the Holy Spirit.

A Low Regeneration Level

In some cases, arrested spiritual development is caused by a low percentage of church members who have been born anew by the power of God. Only the Lord knows how many church members have not made a personal commitment to Jesus Christ. He keeps the Lamb's Book of Life, and he gives none of us access to it. But there is no question that some church members, even some active church members, are not personally reconciled to God through Jesus Christ.

Some churches are more susceptible to this than others. There are people who join a church much as they would join some social club. They need activity. The people there are friendly, the worship services are pleasant, and the sermons are interesting. Children can meet the right kind of friends. And a church member is a very American thing to be. People who have joined the church for these and other similar reasons are present in almost all churches of any denomination.

Across America, statistics show that many people belong to churches, consider themselves active members, and attend church without being born again. Here are the latest Gallup Poll figures among American adults, 18 years of age and over:

102

Church members	68%	102 million
Active members	56%	84 million
Attend church regularly	42%	63 million
Born again	34%	51 million

Probably the 34 percent born-again category is low, according to the Gallup researchers, because some don't use or even understand the term. Some prefer the term "committed to Christ." Some prefer to be called "faithful Christians." But even if the figure were adjusted to compensate for that, there would still be tens of millions of Americans who belong to a church, and who even are active in a church, but who have not been made "new creatures" in Christ Jesus (II Cor. 5:17). All of them are in need of E-0 evangelism, as was defined in chapter 5.

Churches with a high percentage of non-committed members will have arrested spiritual development. They cannot grow normally because, spiritually speaking, they have not yet been born. The people may be church members, but they are not members of the family of God, nor will they be, until they are born again. The answer to such a situation, obviously, is to lead these church members to full commitment to Jesus Christ.

Some people have become specialists in this field. For example, a minister friend of mine, John McClure, feels that his special calling is E-0 evangelism. He will purposely accept a call to a church which has arrested spiritual development and wants to be cured. He loves sharing Christ with people who may have thought that they always had been Christians just because they were church members. In a recent pastorate, he led 150 church members to Christ during his first year there. Then he began to teach them spiritual things, and they matured rapidly. For many years, the church had not grown. The cure took a couple of years, during which time they even lost members. But arrested spiritual development became a thing of the past, and the church grew well. American churches need hundreds more pastors like McClure.

A Low Nurture Level

A large percentage of uncommitted Christians in a church is one form of arrested spiritual development. Another, more prevalent, form is a low level of spiritual nurture among people whose names are already written in the Lamb's Book of Life.

In I Corinthians 3:1, 2, the apostle Paul refers to the Christians in Corinth as "babes in Christ." He is disappointed in them because he says that he could not feed them solid food, but like babies, they could take only milk. Now, milk is good. The human race could not be propagated without it, and the Christian church needs spiritual milk as well. New Christians need the milk of the Word. If they do not receive it, they will have arrested spiritual development and fail to mature in the proper way. Then when they grow up, they can absorb progressively deeper teachings.

A routine part of the diagnosis of the health of a church should be an examination of the spiritual maturity of the members. I will try to list some of the most frequent areas of this kind of need, but in no way do I think that my list will be exhaustive. The factors that can and do contribute to arrested spiritual development are multiple. I will mention eight.

Philosophy of Ministry

Having a well-articulated philosophy of ministry is a sign of strength in a church. This phrase "philosophy of ministry" has not been a common one among church leaders until recently. Few of us learned much about it in seminary. For a time it was thought that churches should be as alike as possible, not as distinct as possible.

But now church leaders are beginning to realize that because unchurched people are so different and have such diverse sets of needs, churches which represent a wide spectrum of philosophies of ministry are able to reach more people and meet more human needs. Thus, many churches are making an effort to articulate their philosophy of ministry so that their own people understand what makes their church different from others, and so that the general public begins to perceive it as well.

One book that describes several alternative philosophies of ministry was recently written by Dan Baumann, pastor of Whittier Area Baptist Fellowship in Whittier, California. He distinguishes, for example, between soul-winning churches, life-situation churches, classroom churches, social action churches, and general practitioner churches. Each one of these types requires a certain kind of pastor, a certain kind of program, and attracts a certain kind of people.

While each of these churches believes that its philosophy of ministry is biblically valid and that by following it they are being true to God and his purposes for them, at the same time they respect other churches that have developed contrasting philosophies of ministry.[1] This seems to me to be a healthy attitude for the body of Christ as a whole.

The philosophy of ministry should be formulated first by the church leadership, but then it must be communicated to the entire congregation. Church members who are unsure of the purpose of their church contribute to arrested spiritual development. In order to avoid this, many churches include their philosophy of ministry as an important component of the curriculum of new members' classes.

Pastoral Care

As has been mentioned several times, the pastor of the church is the key person for that church's health and growth. Although the pastor should not plan to do all the work, he or she has to see that the people are taken care of somehow. The biblical analogy is that of a shepherd and the sheep. Some pastors choose to be ranchers rather than shepherds, but they make sure that the shepherds are also at work. Christian

105

people need counsel, exhortation, guidance in their lives, and support during periods of crisis.

If they are not receiving these things, spiritual development will tend to be retarded. Church membership can become superficial. The function of the church in the minds of the people may become more and more divorced from real life.

The crucial role of the pastor is that of leadership and vision. The pastor, of all people, needs to know where God wants the church to go, and needs to be able to communicate to the members the steps necessary to get there. Churches in the habit of changing pastors every three to six years will usually be deprived of this kind of pastoral ministry, and they will suffer the consequences. Lyle Schaller has found that

> there is overwhelmingly persuasive evidence that from a long-term congregational perspective, the most productive years of a pastorate seldom *begin* before the fourth or fifth or sixth year of a minister's tenure in that congregation.[2]

Almost any minister can baptize, marry, bury, and preach acceptable sermons on Sunday morning. But if the church is interested in long-range health and vigorous growth, it needs to get away from the rapid turnover of ministers characteristic of so many denominations and decide to call a pastor and follow that leadership for an extended period of time. The other alternative is a program-maintaining status quo and perhaps prolonged arrested spiritual development.

The Word of God

Throughout Christian history, the Word of God, the Bible, has been considered the main staple of the Christian's spiritual diet. While I identify with those who emphasize that Bible knowledge without biblical behavior is worthless, nevertheless it is necessary to realize that knowing what God's will is must precede the good Christian deeds. Faith without works is dead, as the Bible affirms (James 2:17), but the order must be faith and then works, never the reverse.

Christian faith is built through the study and application of God's Word. Mature Christians know the Bible, and it is central in their lives. Churches with a "classroom" philosophy of ministry stress this more heavily than most. Typical Sunday sermons are 45- to 50-minute Bible lectures, and the members seem to thrive on them. But every church needs to make sure that somehow or other its members continue to learn more and more about the Bible.

When Bible knowledge is deficient, arrested spiritual development is probable. Church diagnosticians will do well to look at this vital element of Christian life as a possible growth-inhibiting factor.

Personal Piety and Spiritual Formation

A walk with God as a personal dimension in the life of each Christian is of utmost importance. Regular time alone with God in prayer and in the personal study of God's Word builds Christians and helps them in their spiritual formation. While some like to structure this more than others, in one way or another, it must take place. Church members need to be taught how to improve their walk with God.

This relationship with God is a hard aspect of church life to gauge. Perhaps satisfactory measuring instruments will be developed someday, but I have not yet seen any. Personalities differ so much that it is usually not possible to expect people to fit into a mold when it comes to their personal preferences for relating to God. Some churches structure this as a part of their philosophy of ministry and insist on so much time per day in personal devotions. Other churches are freer in this respect. But if somehow or other personal spiritual formation is not taking place, arrested spiritual development may well become a serious church problem.

Spiritual Gifts

Although teaching about spiritual gifts has been increasing across America over the past decade, ignorance of spiritual gifts is still prevalent in many churches. This ignorance is frequently a major contributing factor to arrested spiritual development.

Christians should understand that they are members of a body—the body of Christ. God has placed each of the members in the body as it has pleased him (I Cor. 12:18). Being a bodily member signifies having been assigned a certain function, so when a Christian person discovers his or her spiritual gift, they then understand their function in the body, according to God's plan. Upon discovering the gift or gifts they possess, they find that God provides a supernatural kind of power in using them for his glory and the benefit of the whole body.

When the members know their spiritual gifts, the whole tone of the church improves. It reduces envy and jealousy to a minimum. It mobilizes the membership for the various tasks of the church to maximum efficiency. It removes unnecessary guilt and helps people understand why they can do some things easily and well but not others. It brings joy and fulfillment to individuals. All this is reflected in the general atmosphere of the church and is easily detected by newcomers.

Growing in the use of spiritual gifts is one of the most readily available cures for arrested spiritual development. Tools for making this happen are being developed and refined.[3] They can be used in almost any church where members are committed Christians, although they should be avoided in churches where members are in need of E-0 evangelism.

Fellowship Structures

Church fellowship structures were discussed under koinonitis. Koinonitis occurs when fellowship is overdone.

Arrested spiritual development can occur when fellowship is underdone.

Part of being a Christian and a member of the body of Christ is developing relationships with other Christians. Many churches do not grow because they do not satisfy the deep need for fellowship that men and women have, and that they seek to satisfy when they join the church. Fellowship is a key to assimilating new members.

The two structures where this happens best are the congregation and the cell, as we have defined them previously. Congregations, which have 40 to 120 members, are able to promote social fellowship. Members get to know one another, to know one another's families, to know their vocational involvements, to enjoy mutual interests together, and to share the joys and sorrows of major milestones of life. The cells, which have 8 to 12 members, serve to develop a deeper level of intimacy and mutual accountability. In them a great deal of caring can take place, thus relieving the professional staff of some routine pastoral duties.

It is true that certain churches do not need a well-developed congregational substructure in order to be healthy. In those cases the social fellowship needs of the members are cared for in other ways. By the same token, some groups of church members are not amenable to the cell or small group dynamic. This is not the place to discuss these exceptions to the rule in detail, but it is necessary to point out that the absence of either does not necessarily indicate arrested spiritual development. In many cases, however, it does constitute a defect which needs to be dealt with if the church is going to regain good health.

Worship

All churches worship, but not all churches worship well. Having said this, I need to add that there is no one standard way to worship well. Differing philosophies of ministry demand different styles of worship experiences. But all worship services have a common objective: those who worship must meet God, and his presence must be real to them.

In all too many churches this does not happen. The Sunday morning service is something that must be endured, rather than enjoyed. I must confess that in different periods of my life, I would take a good book to church on Sunday morning and read it on my lap during the service. It was more enjoyable than what was going on around me. But I no longer do that. I am now in a church that gives first priority to worship, and makes it a highlight of the week for church members.

Meaningful worship does not happen automatically, at least here in our contemporary American culture. It has to be developed. Christian people have to be taught to worship. The service needs to be well organized, if it is to bring God and his people together in a special way. I am convinced that many pastors and church leaders do not know enough about worship, nor do many of them realize its importance. When this is the case, a poor worship atmosphere can be a contributing factor to arrested spiritual development and an obstacle to church growth.

Vision for the World

Something special happens in the Christian life when a person sees himself or herself in the context of what God is doing in the whole world. Isolation and introversion occur when church members fail to stretch their vision past their own stained-glass windows. Not only knowing what is going on in the world, but participating in it, brings Christian maturity.

Churches which have developed strong and creative missionary programs have an advantage over those which have not. Recruiting young people for foreign service, and then receiving their reports and their visits during furlough, contribute to a church's health. Generous giving for evangelistic work and for physical, social, and material humanitarian needs builds Christian vitality. Churches are not meant to be centripetal, but centrifugal. A significant part of their ministry needs to be directed toward others.

Introverted and self-seeking Christians are likely to have arrested spiritual development. Building a missionary vision, a concern for the world, and an excitement of sharing with others helps cure it.

The Church Renewal Movement

Many creative ways to reduce arrested spiritual development and free the Holy Spirit for the work among the people of God can be discovered and employed. A group that has specialized in this over the years is the Church Renewal Movement. Church renewal experts came into being to face the challenge of churches which lacked the spiritual maturity for vitality and growth. They have found that the Holy Spirit is quenched in many churches, and that certain new emphases through both clergy and laity are able to renew the body.

When arrested spiritual development is a problem, renewal is essential before the church can grow. It is the remedy for the disease. But two cautions need to be recognized.

First, church renewal is not a cure-all for any church disease, even though it is appropriate to this one. I have seen a church with a serious case of ethnikitis, for example, being treated with large doses of church renewal. Since little improvement resulted, it has caused some to doubt the usefulness of church renewal. But that is like questioning the effectiveness of penicillin because it doesn't cure baldness.

Second, be careful of an overdose of church renewal. An overdose can cause koinonitis and thereby prevent the church from growing well. Churches with arrested spiritual development cannot grow until they are renewed, but they still will not grow if koinonitis is allowed to set in.

111

St. John's Syndrome: How Does a Hot Church Get Lukewarm?

This final disease, like many human diseases, is named for the person who first discovered and described it. Hodgkin's Disease was named for Thomas Hodgkin, Parkinson's Disease was named for James Parkinson, and St. John's Syndrome is named for the apostle John. He described it in the well-known passage containing the letters to the seven churches in Asia Minor, in Revelation, chapters two and three.

The underlying problem of St. John's Syndrome is Christian nominality. When Christians become Christians in name only, when they feel that their faith is only routine, when church involvement is largely going through the motions, and when belonging to church is a family tradition and a social nicety, St. John's Syndrome is likely at work.

Church Life Cycles

Churches, like people, tend to go through life cycles, although there is a difference. The human life cycle is inevitable. There is no such thing as a fountain of youth. But the church life cycle is not inevitable. Decline, weakness, and death can be avoided if St. John's Syndrome is understood, and if steps are taken to prevent it.

David Moberg, one of America's foremost sociologists of religion, describes the church life cycle in five stages: (1) the incipient organization, (2) the formal organization, (3) the stage of maximum efficiency, (4) the institutional stage, and (5) disintegration.[1] St. John's Syndrome sets in during the institutional stage.

The phenomenon of St. John's Syndrome can be pictured by drawing a bell curve on a piece of graph paper. If the vertical axis is church membership, and the horizontal axis is time, the typical pattern will look like a bell. The usual configuration is as follows: (1) Rapid growth. This is the upcurve on the left hand side of the bell; (2) Plateau. This is when the curve begins to form the top of the bell; (3) Decline. This is the right hand side of the bell on its downward curve; (4) Stagnation. Finally the curve flattens out at a low membership figure, and the church learns simply how to survive. After that, another disease such as ethnikitis might set in and finish off the church.

Although the time required for this to happen will vary from church to church, a common pattern is for the rapid-growth period to last about 20 years, the plateau for the next 10 years, and the decline from the thirtieth year onward.

These time sequences seemed to be confirmed by a very interesting study conducted by Douglas Walrath on Reformed Church in America churches in the Albany, New York, area. Walrath developed a typology of churches and did what is called a "quadratic regression study" on the churches of each type. Many of his graphs look precisely like the St. John's Syndrome bell curve we have been describing. Unfortunately, this research has not yet been published, but it does give some empirical indication that this is what needs to be looked out for in churches that intend to maintain a good growth rate.

Lukewarm Churches

Forty years was just about the length of time needed for the decline to set in among the first-century churches in Asia

113

Minor. Their beginning is described in Acts 19. Paul was on his third term as a missionary, and he stayed in the area longer than he had stayed at any other place. People not only in the city of Ephesus, but all over Asia Minor, were open to the preaching of Jesus Christ, and a number of churches were started.

It was an exciting time. The churches were in their first stages of rapid growth. Public debates were being held. The synagogue split. Evil spirits were being cast out. Believers were speaking with tongues and prophesying. People were being healed of their diseases. Animists were finding Christ and burning their fetishes, one pile of which was said to be worth 50,000 pieces of silver or about $10,000. Because their business had taken a nosedive, the silversmiths rioted. Few would buy the idols they were manufacturing.

Ephesus was the center of evangelistic work for the whole district. From there Paul and the other members of his apostolic band spread the gospel until "all they which dwelt in Asia heard the word of the Lord Jesus, both Jews and Greeks" (Acts 19:10).

Forty years later, however, the church was in a different condition. St. John's Syndrome had set in. To read John's account of the church at Ephesus in Revelation is saddening. Nothing is said there about animists burning fetishes or people being healed or silversmiths rioting or new converts being added to the church daily. The flames of evangelism had died down to a flicker, and the church was said to have left its "first love" (Rev. 2:4).

It had become a second-generation church. The cost of becoming a Christian was minimal for those who had been brought up in Christian families. When the parents had become Christians, they were threatened and castigated. When the children became Christians, they received a smile and a pat on the back. They were neither cold nor hot, but lukewarm (Rev. 3:15, 16).

As one reads through the letters to the seven churches,

several particular symptoms are mentioned. The "doctrine of Balaam" (Rev. 2:14), for example, may have been a reduction of strictness in the church through intermarriage with the heathen people. Although the intermarriage problem is more acute in some situations than in others, the need to maintain strictness is very important for a religious organization that wants to grow, as Dean Kelley has shown in his book *Why Conservative Churches Are Growing*.

Another is the "doctrine of the Nicolaitans" (Rev. 2:15). This may have meant the imposition of the rule of the clergy over the laity in the church, since the root words are *nikaō* which means "to conquer" and *laos* which means "the people." If it does signify clericalism, this is known to be a problem among churches today that have St. John's Syndrome. In chapter one, we argued that one of the axioms of church growth is that the people must want their church to grow and be willing to pay the price. They must be ready and willing to commit themselves—their time, energy, and money—to growth. They should be discovering, developing, and using their spiritual gifts. Pastors who decide to do it all themselves usually do not stimulate growth dynamics.

Although it is not necessary here to continue to list in detail the problems of the churches in first-century Asia Minor, one more should be mentioned because it is so frequently associated with St. John's Syndrome. This is affluence produced by redemption and lift. The church at Laodicea was rich and comfortable, but spiritually poor (Rev. 3:17). Poorer people, who through their commitment to Christ develop upward social mobility, can find themselves cut off from their own friends and relatives. This can be a part of St. John's Syndrome. While there is nothing intrinsically wrong with affluence, if upward mobility cuts Christian people off from the opportunity of winning those from their own social group to Christ, it can halt growth. In extreme cases, such as the one described in James 2, people in upward mobility can even come to *despise* their former peers. What needs to be

115

understood is that affluence, in certain circumstances, can be a growth problem for churches.

Within 40 years the churches in Asia Minor, once very much alive spiritually, were considered dead (Rev. 3:1). They were still surviving as social institutions, but because of St. John's syndrome, their former vitality had been sapped away, and therefore they were a disappointment to God.

St. John's Syndrome in Relation to Other Diseases

St. John's Syndrome relates in particular to two of the other diseases—arrested spiritual development and old age.

The symptoms of St. John's Syndrome can be similar to those of arrested spiritual development, and often are. St. John's Syndrome, however, relates specifically to the nominality that can infect a church when the second generation comes along. Because of such nominality, the spiritual development of that generation is frequently arrested, so the two diseases relate. But it seems that the value of examining a church in terms of its life cycle is high enough to merit a separate category of disease instead of attempting to combine the two.

Old age and St. John's Syndrome are more distinct, but in certain circumstances they may be confused. The essential difference is that old age is caused by local contextual factors and St. John's Syndrome by local institutional factors, as these terms were explained in chapter 1. Sometimes a declining church may be observed that has a high percentage of senior citizens who are wonderful Christian people, but it does not seem to be attracting new members. In fact, the people in this hypothetical church do not want it to grow, and the clear indication is that the church will die with that generation. But if this is happening in a community that is not itself deteriorating, the church by definition does not have old age. The cause of its problem may be koinonitis, but it is more likely to be St. John's Syndrome.

Leaving the First Love

St. John writes in Revelation 2:4 that Jesus had something against the church in Ephesus because it had left its first love.

Both exegetes and homileticians can have a field day with this phrase, because we are not told definitely what the first love of the church at Ephesus actually was. Some interpret it as brotherly love, some interpret it as love for God. I, however, see it as a love for lost men and women in need of reconciliation to God. If the church at Ephesus was anything, it was a center of evangelism. Paul stayed there for three years, and Ephesus became his second base for missionary work, with Antioch being the first. His intention after the three years was to move to a third base, Rome, and for that reason he wrote the Epistle to the Romans right after his stay in Ephesus. It seems from Acts 19, that the church at Ephesus was the mother church of all the other churches in Asia Minor. It was growing both by expansion and by extension.

Such an expression of love and concern for those who are not saved is a common characteristic of a new church still in its early stage of rapid growth. The current growth line is the left side of the bell curve. It exists for others, not for itself, and as a result, God blesses, and the church grows. Evangelism is the top outreach priority of such a church, as it was in Ephesus.

A growth problem is bound to arise when the outreach priorities are switched. This has nothing to do with other kinds of priorities, such as commitment to Christ and commitment to the body of Christ, both of which I believe need to precede outreach. But if a church that is otherwise in good health allows nominality to dim its belief that people without God have no hope, either in this world or in the world to come, and if the church does not act on this belief with aggressive evangelism, St. John's Syndrome has taken its toll.

Evangelism, of course, is only a facet of the totality of God's mission in the world. The cultural mandate stands tall alongside the evangelistic mandate. Jesus told us to love our

117

neighbor as ourselves (Matt. 22:39). Christian social concerns need to be, and are, widely expressed in the world. Jesus said:

> The Spirit of the Lord is upon me, because he hath anointed me to preach the gospel to the poor; he hath sent me to heal the brokenhearted, to preach deliverance to the captives, and recovering of sight to the blind. (Luke 4:18, 19)

The cultural mandate is not optional for biblical Christians.

The evangelistic mandate, however, looks at human beings in a slightly different way. It does not see people so much as naked or clothed, hungry or full, oppressed or liberated. It sees people rather as lost or saved, condemned or justified, estranged or reconciled. Both ways of looking at people partially reflect God's perspective.

The Priority of Evangelism

While both evangelism and social concern are parts of the mission of the church in the world, evangelism is the top priority. As the Lausanne Covenant affirms, "In the church's mission of sacrificial service evangelism is primary." I fully realize that some will read this and disagree. They feel that the two emphases ought to be equal, or even that social concern should be supreme. Their Christian compassion is commendable, but they should realize they are suggesting a formula which predictably will cause churches to plateau and decline.

Some of the mainline churches in America have discovered this recently. Over the past decade, as we have noted in chapter 1, the United Methodists lost over one million members and the United Presbyterians, a half million. The severe decline began in the middle of the sixties. Special task forces have been named by these denominations to try to uncover the problems that have caused the decline.

The reports that have been written conclude first of all that church growth is complex. In no case can a simplistic, generalized reason explain why churches grow or decline. But as I understand the reports, they do confirm that taking strong stands for social concern, to the detriment of carrying out the evangelistic mandate, is one of the major causes of church decline in America. It is, in a word, losing its first love.

It is easy to see why this could have happened in the sixties. The Vietnam war, the civil rights movement, the development of a hippie counterculture, the death-of-God movement—all combined to stir the nation to its core. Church bureaucrats, like other Americans, felt these problems deeply, and they used their influence to do their part to heal society. In the process, they produced a change in priorities that eventually affected the churches at the grassroots, so that they began to lose members.

Sociological studies have shown that members left mainline churches taking strong social positions, not because the churches became socially involved, but because in doing so, the churches had relegated evangelism to a secondary position. In one of the preliminary studies commissioned by the National Council of Churches, Douglas Johnson and George Cornell say:

> Summing up, America's churches are chiefly dedicated to that old-time endeavor that never gets old, spreading the Gospel. . . . Whether they see it in terms of prayer or evangelism, however, it is considered the local church's central imperative by Christians across the continent, black and white, city folks and back countrymen.[2]

When the average Christian person, or non-Christian person, for that matter, perceives that a church is giving evangelism anything other than top priority in its outreach ministry, the church is perceived to be weak and unattractive. Churches that wish to avoid the decline represented by the right-hand side of St. John's Syndrome bell curve need to take steps to avoid allowing this to happen.

If they do, they might be surprised to find that when they give evangelism first priority, they end up doing more and

119

better social work. The Gallup poll recently tested this by comparing the social involvement of evangelical churches, which usually give the evangelistic mandate priority, to that of other churches, which are more likely to treat it as secondary. They found that 42 percent of the evangelicals are involved in helping the poor, the sick, the handicapped, and the elderly, compared to only 26 percent of the nonevangelical Christians.

Preventing St. John's Syndrome

The best approach to St. John's Syndrome is preventive, rather than therapeutic, medicine. It is much easier to avoid it than to get over it. In fact, getting over it might require a cure similar to that of ethnikitis—a complete blood transfusion. That in itself is probably not so much curing the disease as dying with dignity.

St. John's Syndrome, however, has a sure-fire prevention. Because it is largely a disease of second generation Christians, it can be prevented by making sure that there is always a healthy number of first generation Christians in the church. Like koinonitis, it can be prevented or cured by steady conversion growth. Biological growth alone tends to produce St. John's Syndrome. Transfer growth may or may not help. If the people transferring in are nominal Christians, it will not help. But new Christians freshly converted, babes in Christ who soon grow and mature and reproduce themselves, will keep the church healthy, vigorous, and growing, as long as the supply lasts.

Conclusion

There undoubtedly will be other diseases which church pathologists will add to ethnikitis, old age, people-blindness, hyper-cooperativism, koinonitis, sociological strangulation, arrested spiritual development, and St. John's Syndrome. I have seen suggestions such as "Laodecian lethargy," "acute doctrinitis," "indifferentism," "absolutism," "hardening of the categories," "formalism," and others. One that I myself have considered adding is "premature birth." But in this concluding section, I must express two sincere hopes.

1. I hope that the eight names will be accepted, now that they are in print. I realize that many people will not like the names. I can't say that I like them too well either. But who likes cystic fibrosis or encephalitis or trichinosis or Chaggas' disease or even Russian flu? If these names were changed every time a new book of pathology was written, medical science would be a shambles. I hope church pathology will not fall into that trap.

2. I hope that new diseases will be added only with a great deal of caution. I'm sure the list can and will be expanded by others, and I welcome this. I have tried to describe diseases which are not limited to any one Protestant tradition, but which apply quite generally, at least to Anglo-American churches. Whether they apply to other cultures as well, only time will tell. But the list was not made out hastily. Each one of the diseases does have a discernible relationship to church growth and decline. It is my hope that as the list expands, these factors will be given full consideration.

My conviction is that God wants his church, the body of Christ, healthy, and that if it is healthy, it will grow. Ephesians 4:13 expresses the desire that "we all come in the unity of the faith, and of the knowledge of the Son of God, unto a perfect man, unto the measure of the stature of the fulness of Christ." This kind of maturity produces church growth, and as verse 16 says: "So when each separate part works as it should, the whole body grows" (TEV).

Notes

Chapter 1

1. David A. Roozen, *Church Membership and Participation: Trends, Determinants and Implications for Policy and Planning* (Hartford: Hartford Seminary Foundation, 1978). Also, Jackson W. Carroll, "The Church in the World," *Theology Today* (April 1978), pp. 70-80.

2. Examples of such interdenominational "ecclesiologists" are Lyle E. Schaller of the Yokefellow Institute, 530 N. Brainard, Naperville, Illinois 60540, and the staff of Fuller Evangelistic Association's Department of Church Growth, Box 989, Pasadena, California 91102, under the direction of Carl George.

3. For example, over 100 pastors are being currently trained in diagnostic procedures each year in the Fuller Seminary Doctor of Ministry Program, 135 North Oakland Ave., Pasadena, California 91101.

4. C. Peter Wagner, *Your Church Can Grow* (Glendale: Regal Books, 1976).

5. C. Peter Wagner, *Your Spiritual Gifts Can Help Your Church Grow* (Glendale: Regal Books, 1979).

6. Howard L. Rice, "Foreword," in Foster H. Shannon, *The Growth Crisis in the American Church* (Pasadena, William Carey Library, 1977), p. xii.

7. As one way that has been proved effective in motivating a congregation for growth, I recommend the ten-hour Basic Growth Seminars conducted by the staff of the Institute for American Church Growth, 150 S. Los Robles Ave., Suite 600, Pasadena, California 91101, under the direction of Win Arn.

Chapter 2

1. Elaine Furlow, "Choices Amid Changes?" *Home Missions* (September 1975), pp. 34-36.

2. Walter E. Ziegenhals, "Austin's 'New' Church," *The Christian Ministry* (November 1976), pp. 5-9.

3. "UCC's Covenants for Churches in Change," *Christian Century* (November 16, 1977), p. 1055.

Chapter 3

1. The story of Zion Church was taken from an item in *The Covenant Companion* (January 1, 1977), p. 18.

2. William H. Willimon, "Pastoral Care of Dying Churches," *The Christian Ministry* (March 1978), pp. 27-30.

3. For an attempt at standardizing diagnostic procedures see the *Diagnostic Clinic* produced by Fuller Evangelistic Association, P. O. Box 989, Pasadena, California 91102.

Chapter 4

1. Ralph D. Winter, "The Highest Priority: Cross-Cultural Evangelism," J. D. Douglas, ed., *Let the Earth Hear His Voice* (Minneapolis: World Wide Publishers, 1975), pp. 213-25.

2. The data for this example are taken from *Tie Lines* (Vol. 6, Nos. 1, 3, 1976), a newsletter published by the Department of Church Extension of the Bible Fellowship Church.

3. Charles E. Mylander, *Suburban Friends Growth* (Pasadena: Fuller Theological Seminary, unpublished doctoral dissertation, 1975), p. 10.

Chapter 5

1. See, for example, Donald McGavran, *Understanding Church Growth* (Grand Rapids: Eerdmans, 1970), pp. 31-48; Wagner, *Your Church Can Grow*, pp. 161-71.

2. This research was reported in Win C. Arn, "A Church Growth Look at Here's Life America," *Church Growth: America* (Jan.-Feb. 1977), pp. 4 ff.; and C. Peter Wagner, "Who Found It?" *Eternity* (September 1977), pp. 13-19.

3. Lyle E. Schaller, "Reflections on Cooperative Ministries," *The Clergy Journal* (September 1977), p. 21.

Chapter 6

1. This is described in C. Peter Wagner, *What Are We Missing?* (Carol Stream: Creation House, 1978), p. 42.

2. Edward E. Plowman, "The Deepening Rift in the Charismatic Movement," *Christianity Today* (October 10, 1975), p. 52.

3. Gottfried Oosterwal, *Patterns of SDA Church Growth in North America* (Berrien Springs, Mich.: Andrews University Press), pp. 51, 52.

Chapter 7

1. Robert H. Schuller, *Your Church Has Real Possibilities* (Glendale: Regal Books, 1974), pp. 20, 21.

Chapter 8

1. Dan Baumann, *All Originality Makes a Dull Church* (Santa Ana, California: Vision House, 1976).

2. Lyle E. Schaller, *Assimilating New Members* (Nashville, Abingdon, 1978), p. 53.

3. For a comprehensive treatment of this, see Wagner, *Your Spiritual Gifts Can Help Your Church Grow.*

An excellent practical workshop for discovering the gifts designed for church groups is available from Fuller Evangelistic Association, Box 989, Pasadena, California 91102.

Chapter 9

1. David O. Moberg, *The Church as a Social Institution* (Englewood Cliffs: Prentice Hall, 1962), pp. 118-23.

2. Douglas W. Johnson and George W. Cornell, *Punctured Preconceptions* (New York: Friendship Press, 1972), p. 108.

Index

124

Your Church Can Be Healthy